THE STOIC ARSENAL

THE STOIC ARSENAL

*40 Lessons from Stoicism
for a Better Life*

―⚬⚬⚬―

Leandro Faria

LUMINARE PRESS
WWW.LUMINAREPRESS.COM

The Stoic Arsenal: 40 Lessons from Stoicism for a Better Life
Copyright © 2021 by Leandro Faria

All rights reserved. This book or any portion thereof may not be reproduced or used in any manner whatsoever without the express written permission of the publisher, except for the use of brief quotations in a book review.

Printed in the United States of America

Luminare Press
442 Charnelton St.
Eugene, OR 97401
www.luminarepress.com

LCCN: 2021916520
ISBN: 978-1-64388-731-9

TABLE OF CONTENTS

Acknowledgments 1
Introduction 3

PART 1
Life Is Only Perception

Lesson 1: Mens Omnia Regit 15
Lesson 2: Train Perception 21
Lesson 3: Override Initial Reactions 26
Lesson 4: Trichotomy of Control 31
Lesson 5: Mindfulness 36
Lesson 6: The Inner Citadel 40

PART 2
Keep Perspective

Lesson 7: Amor Fati 47
Lesson 8: Cosmic Perspective 51
Lesson 9: Break the Hedonic Treadmill 55
Lesson 10: Memento Mori 59
Lesson 11: Fair Bookkeeping 65
Lesson 12: Poverty Is a State of Mind 69

PART 3
Downside Protection

Lesson 13: Wand of Hermes 77
Lesson 14: Premeditatio Malorum 83

Lesson 15: Fate Only Lends 88
Lesson 16: Self-Denial 93
Lesson 17: Decatastrophize 99
Lesson 18: Change the Point of View 106

PART 4
Sympatheia

Lesson 19: Cosmopolitanism 115
Lesson 20: We're More Similar than Different 120
Lesson 21: Forgive Wrongs of Others 126
Lesson 22: Focus on Virtues, Not Flaws 133
Lesson 23: Improve Others 138
Lesson 24: Show Appreciation 143
Lesson 25: Character Is All That Matters 150

PART 5
Pragmatism

Lesson 26: Stop Complaining 159
Lesson 27: Don't Seek Recognition 164
Lesson 28: Don't Seek Happiness 169
Lesson 29: Choose Friends Wisely 175
Lesson 30: Have a Sense of Humor 180
Lesson 31: Control Your Anger 188
Lesson 32: Be Humble 197

PART 6
Practice

Lesson 33: Philosophy Takes Priority 205
Lesson 34: Learn for Yourself 209
Lesson 35: Excellence Is a Habit 214

Lesson 36: Actions, Not Words 222
Lesson 37: Protect Your Time 227
Lesson 38: Watch the Wise 234
Lesson 39: The Power of Reminders 240
Lesson 40: Create a New Path 247

Selected Bibliography 253

Acknowledgments

1. The team at Luminare Press
   For all the advice, suggestions, comments, edits, and the innumerous details necessary to get a book ready for publishing.

2. Colleen Vanderlinden
   For the kind words of encouragement and help with the initial manuscript.

3. Ryan Holiday, William Irvine, Massimo Pigliucci, Ward Farnsworth
   For promoting Stoicism in the modern world. For the excellent work that served as inspiration for this book.

4. Donald Robertson
   For the immense contributions to the world of contemporary Stoicism. For the invaluable manuscript advice.

5. Ivan Biava
   For the commitment to making Stoicism available to broader audiences. For the exchange of ideas and manuscript assistance.

6. Andrea, Thomas, Juliana
   For being the reason why I seek to be a better person.

Introduction

1. Realization. Some experiences forever change the way we perceive the world. I'll never forget the alarm clock ringing at 4:45 a.m. on a cold November night. The temperature outside was 19 degrees Fahrenheit. We were about thirty minutes away from the park, and the hike to the top of the mountain would take around one hour. As long as we left soon, we shouldn't have any problems reaching the top before sunrise, which according to the forecast would be at 7:06 a.m.

I hated hiking. In the mind of a young college student, waking up before dawn to hike up a mountain in the freezing cold was a cruel punishment. That was the whole point. I was rushing a fraternity, and this was an initiation event. We were supposed to report back with a picture of the sunrise taken from the top of the mountain. I accepted it as the price to pay for admittance and headed along with the other poor souls being subjected to the ordeal.

When we arrived at the park, I noticed something unexpected. About half of the group had an attitude of silent acceptance and dissatisfaction. I was part of this group. But the other half appeared to be excited. They actually looked forward to the hike. They eagerly grabbed their backpacks and walked straight to the trail. I couldn't understand how anyone could act that way given the annoying task we'd been given. I just kept quiet and followed them on the dark, wooded path. One hour later, we had completed the mission successfully. It was time to head back to the fraternity headquarters for debriefing. What happened at headquarters completely shocked me.

We were greeted by a large group. They asked us to show the picture of the sunrise, which we immediately did. The guy who was the fraternity president must have felt like he should say something. He made an unassuming comment: "This was my favorite event when I rushed." About half of those around him thought he was being sarcastic and laughed. He was taken aback by the reaction. "What's funny about that?" One of his closer friends replied: "Come on, we know you're joking. This is a hazing event. Nobody likes it." I noticed more confused faces pop up. "Hazing? What hazing? This is supposed to be a fun bonding activity." The person who had organized the event decided to chime in: "It is clearly hazing." At that point, everyone's expressions had morphed into sheer confusion. The group started dividing itself into two equally sized camps. My half was convinced that the event was hazing. How could it not be? Who wants to wake up before sunrise to go hike in freezing weather? To my surprise, a lot of people do. The other half looked at us like we were aliens. They were perplexed by our take on the situation. How could we think that going on a beautiful hike in nature and watching the sunrise from the best view in town was hazing? From their standpoint, we should be thankful for the opportunity.

This experience had a profound effect on me. It was the first time that I reflected on the power of perspective. Obviously, I had realized before that people could have differing opinions on a specific topic. The opposing views weren't what captured my attention. What struck me was that, in my head, I had just spent a miserable morning walking around in the cold trying to get admitted to a stupid fraternity I wasn't fully sold on anyway. But to several other people who were there with me, the morning had been great. This was the thought that blew my mind: I had subjected myself to unnecessary suffering. My judgment of events had led me to think of the situation as hardship. The difference between my terrible morning and their memorable one was purely the way we had perceived it.

My realization made me wonder how often this occurred. How many times during the past week had I made myself suffer over something that could've been a source of joy? How many times over the past month? Year? My entire life? It was overwhelming to think of the cumulative toll of all those negative experiences. How much suffering could've been avoided by just looking at things differently? And most of my life was still ahead of me. I didn't want to set sail in turbulent waters if a calmer route was available. Was there something out there that could assist me in the journey? It was the beginning of the search that led me to Stoicism.

2. *Philosophy.* Anyone who embarks on an introspective journey runs into the topic of philosophy at some point. Initially, I approached it with a negative bias. The philosophy classes I had taken in college had focused almost exclusively on highly technical deliberations. I hadn't extracted much value from discussing term arrangements in prosleptic syllogisms. These negative experiences made me develop a cynical attitude toward the subject. Luckily, I was introduced to the book *Philosophy as a Way of Life* by French philosopher Pierre Hadot (more about him in lesson 6). His book was a breath of fresh air. Hadot argued that philosophy had lost touch with its original purpose. In the ancient world, the purpose of philosophy was to help people live better lives. Only in recent times had it become the recondite and excessively academic subject I associated it with. Hadot was highly critical of the "scholasticism" of philosophy, which had created an isolated world where technicians trained technicians in subjects that no one outside of academia cared about.

> *One of the characteristics of the university is that it is made up of professors who train professors, or professionals who train professionals. Education was thus no longer directed toward people who were to become educated with a view to becoming fully developed human beings, but to specialists, in order that they might train other specialists. [...] In modern university philosophy, philosophy is obviously no longer a way of life or form of life unless it be the form of life of a professor of philosophy.*
>
> Pierre Hadot,
Philosophy as a Way of Life,
Chapter 11

Pierre Hadot specialized in ancient Greco-Roman philosophy. He was an avid admirer of Stoicism, which led me to read a Stoic text for the first time. It was Letter 48 from Seneca's *Moral Epistles*, in which Seneca mocks philosophy that is excessively academic.

> 'Mouse is a syllable, and a syllable does not nibble cheese; therefore, a mouse does not nibble cheese.' What childish fatuities these are! Is this what philosophers acquire wrinkles in brows for? Is this what we let our beards grow long for? Is this what we teach with faces grave and pale? Shall I tell you what philosophy holds out to humanity? Counsel. One person is facing death, another is vexed by poverty, while another is tormented by wealth—whether his own or someone else's; one man is appalled by his misfortunes while another longs to get away from his own prosperity; one man is suffering at the hands of men, another at the hands of the gods. What's the point of concocting whimsies for me of the sort I've just been mentioning?
>
> Seneca,
Moral Epistles, Letter 48

This was the beginning of my interest in Stoicism. Hadot's idea of "philosophy as a way of life" was appealing to me. I was looking for something that could serve as a guide in day-to-day situations. According to Hadot, Stoicism was a philosophy of life that could provide that. The text by Seneca made me curious to learn more.

3. *Eudaimonia*. So that's the story of how I reached Stoicism. Now I'll describe what convinced me it is valuable. The short answer is quite simple: Stoicism is valuable because it works. And it works because it was created with a clear purpose: to help the practitioner achieve *eudaimonia*. What does this mean? *Eudaimonia* is a Greek term that has been translated as "well-being," "human flourishing," or "life-satisfaction." It is a nuanced term without an exact translation in English, but the core idea is that it describes a state

of thorough satisfaction with life, not a quick rush of happiness. *Eudaimonia* is closer to "living a good life" than "feeling happy in the moment." Therefore, Stoicism was created to help people live a good life. I always appreciated the straightforwardness of that objective. I've seen some writers claim that the end goal of a Stoic is to live a life of virtuous action. In my opinion, this is a misunderstanding. The goal is to live a good life—to reach *eudaimonia*. Acting virtuously is the path that gets us there. When we get on an airplane, our goal is to reach our destination, not to just fly.

Living a good life is a unanimous and uncontested objective. Few people would argue that it isn't worth pursuing. But how does Stoicism get us there? Why is it effective in this pursuit? It all starts with a fundamental claim made by Stoicism: we can achieve *eudaimonia* by training our minds. According to Stoic philosophy, the key to a good life lies within us. This notion contradicts many Western schools of thought, which assert that human well-being is derived extrinsically—from sources placed outside of ourselves. Based on this view, a good life is a result of external factors such as money, fame, praise, success, or even the effects that supernatural beings exert over us. Stoicism takes the opposite position: well-being is derived intrinsically, from the quality of our mind. If we assume that the Stoic argument is correct, then we conclude that the key to living a good life is ensuring that our mind is healthy.

4. *The mind.* The human brain has been described as the most complex object in the known universe. Our understanding of it is still very rudimentary, but the little that we already know has given us glimpses into how it operates. We know that the human mind is the result of an evolutionary process. Our thought patterns are the way they are because this specific mind configuration increased the evolutionary fitness of our ancestors. These ancestors had a higher likelihood of procreating due to the way their minds operated. The human mind wasn't selected for maximizing *eudaimonia*. It was selected for maximizing evolutionary fitness. Therefore, we aren't optimized for flourishing. Our brains carry around a software that

was picked based on its ability to make our ancestors have children before dying. Whether they lived fulfilling lives was somewhat irrelevant.

The ancient Stoics were unaware of this story of our origins. But they realized that our minds routinely give us something different from what we desire. We seek a happy life, but we are given all types of emotions that make us unhappy. The Stoics could tell that *eudaimonia* wouldn't just come about naturally—it would require a way of training the mind. Epictetus lectured his students about this. He defined a wise person as one who is always on alert against himself.

> *[The wise man] keeps an eye on himself as if he were his own enemy lying in wait.*
>
> Epictetus,
> *Enchiridion, Chapter 48*

A philosophy of life is so incredibly important because of this savage nature of the mind. Without philosophy, you will navigate through life guided by evolutionary urges, without much control of the path. We become puppets of our feelings, which are generated by a mind that wasn't designed to produce well-being. To make it worse, this problem is magnified by modern technology. The stimuli we're subjected to is always changing, causing an evolutionary mismatch between what our bodies were designed for and the environment we live in. The great accomplishment of the Stoic teachers of the past millennia was to develop a collection of teachings that help us domesticate our thoughts. Stoic theory proposes a framework to view the world and process the information we're subjected to. It provides deep observations about how the mind works and uses these lessons to create a mechanism that allows us to reclaim ourselves. Stoicism gives us a repository of advice, mental techniques, and exercises that can help its practitioners to live better lives. This repository is what I refer to as "The Stoic Arsenal."

5. *Validation.* I'm a skeptic by nature. My skepticism makes it difficult for me to fully endorse something. Some of my acquaintances think that my appreciation for Stoicism is somewhat out of character. My response to that comment is the following: nothing is 100 percent certain. Scientific inquiry is predicated on the idea that all we have are hypotheses. We believe that some hypotheses are more likely than others to be true. At a certain point, for practical purposes, we start treating those hypotheses as truth. As an example, we believe that our universe is dictated by sequential events that follow a cause-and-effect relationship. A domino falls because another one hits it. A ball moves because someone throws it. We've seen enough examples to treat this as true. But from the standpoint of the scientific method, even something as basic as cause-and-effect is still a hypothesis open to inquiry. It could be that we have a fundamental misunderstanding of the nature of our universe, and that we actually live in a teleological universe, where things are being pulled by the future as opposed to moving into it. This would mean that our cause-and-effect hypothesis is incorrect. The effect is what drives the cause, and not the other way around. This example might sound outlandish, but human history records many episodes of "absolute truths" being proven to be incorrect. The point I'm trying to make is that there is a greater than zero percent chance that Stoicism is just a bunch of nonsense. But I've personally seen and experienced enough to believe that it is effective in its goal of helping a practitioner live a better life. I believe that there are objective and subjective arguments in its favor.

Let's start with the main objective argument. Stoicism served as the basis for development of cognitive behavioral therapy (CBT). This type of psychotherapy is fully sanctioned by the American Psychological Association (APA). Almost 90 percent of the psychotherapeutic techniques considered empirically supported by the APA come from CBT. Cognitive behavioral therapy is utilized by the majority of licensed therapists in the United States, and all psychiatry residents are mandated to receive training in it. The

American psychiatrist Aaron T. Beck, regarded as the father of CBT, wrote about the influence of Stoicism in his seminal work *Cognitive Therapy of Depression*.

> *The philosophical origins of cognitive therapy can be traced back to Stoic philosophers.*
>
> AARON T. BECK, A. JOHN RUSH,
> BRIAN F. SHAW, GARY EMERY,
> *Cognitive Therapy of Depression*, Chapter 1

Stoicism's association to CBT makes it the most scientifically scrutinized philosophy of mind in history. Many of the core Stoic mental techniques have undergone clinical study and validation in the process of receiving APA endorsement. I've told several people that they can choose their preferred way of learning Stoicism: they can learn it now, on their own, or later, from the mouth of a therapist.

Now, moving on to more subjective arguments. In my opinion, Stoicism is effective because of the emphasis it places on an important facet of human psychology. There is an asymmetry of preference that is evolutionarily baked into the human mind. We are wired to avoid suffering more than we seek well-being. Consider a hypothetical experiment where you are given two alternatives: Option A consists of spending the next hour under "normal" circumstances. You will just carry on with your life, and nothing out of the ordinary will happen. Option B is composed of thirty minutes of the most incredible bliss a human being could possibly experience, followed by thirty minutes of the most extreme suffering imaginable. If given these two choices, most people would select Option A. People are afraid of Option B because of the thirty minutes of suffering. Our brains are hardwired to perceive pleasure and pain asymmetrically: we fear pain more than we seek pleasure. This idea is supported by modern psychological research. Given this feature of the mind, it makes sense that a philosophy designed to pursue well-being would place special emphasis on mitigating psychological pain. I believe that Stoicism provides the most comprehensive tool set to deal with hardship out of any philosophy I've encountered.

Another pro-Stoic argument that I value highly is related to its functional nature. Stoicism is effective because it is feasible to practice. The most notable Stoic teachers in history weren't isolated monks meditating in front of a waterfall. They were people with busy schedules. They had family matters to attend to. They had jobs. They were subject to misfortune in their lives. In sum: they were real people. Stoicism was custom made for an active routine. It was designed to help the day-to-day lives of real people. The Stoic lessons described in this book can be incorporated into anyone's schedule without causing much disturbance. This practical nature of Stoicism makes it more likely that someone will embrace it.

6. *Conclusion.* *The Stoic Arsenal* is meant to be a collection of the Stoic lessons that I found to be the most helpful. I don't have an academic background in philosophy. I don't read the Stoic texts like a professor looking for philosophical abstractions. I read Stoicism in search of self-betterment. I'm not interested in the arguments about epistemology that were common in the early period of Greek Stoicism. I respect and appreciate the academics who focus on this topic, but it isn't my area of interest. The teachings included in this book are mostly derived from the late Stoicism that was practiced in the Roman Empire, which put more emphasis on ethics and human psychology. These texts are surprisingly accessible and easy to follow. They hold all the value contained in *The Stoic Arsenal*. My role as the author is equivalent to that of a color-commentator in a sports broadcast: I have tried to provide some structure while allowing the superstars to make the real impact. My hope is that the readers of this book—whether beginners or experts in Stoic philosophy—find it useful as an everyday guide for better living. Stoicism improved the quality of my life; I'm confident it can do the same for you.

Part 1

LIFE IS ONLY PERCEPTION

---

*Keep this refuge in mind:
Things have no hold on the soul. They stand there
unmoving, outside it. Disturbances come only
from within—from our own perceptions.
Our life is only perception.*

MARCUS AURELIUS,
Meditations, 4.3

Lesson 1

MENS OMNIA REGIT

The mind rules over everything.

There is an inscription near the entrance of the Nicolaus Copernicus museum in Frombork, Poland, that states in bold letters: *Sol Omnia Regit*. The Latin phrase translates to "the sun rules over everything." It is a fitting caption in a museum honoring the father of heliocentrism. It is undeniably true that from the standpoint of astrophysics, the sun is the absolute ruler of our immediate astronomical vicinity. It accounts for 99.8 percent of the mass of our solar system. But the sun doesn't determine whether we live happy lives. Our anxieties, fears, and frustrations aren't caused by the sun. For an individual, what rules over everything isn't something in the sky but something that resides much closer. The center of our existence resides in the human brain, which gives rise to what we refer to as the *mind*.

The Stoics understood very well that for a human being, it is the mind that rules everything: *Mens Omnia Regit*. The mind is the key to the quality of life we experience. The only difference between a good and a bad day is the lens through which it is viewed. Aaron T. Beck, the father of cognitive behavioral therapy, and considered one of the most influential psychiatrists of all time, was heavily influenced by Stoicism. He utilized an analogy of colored glasses to explain the power of the mind. According to him, we can look at the world through happy, rose-tinted glasses or sad, blue-tinted ones.

But it would be a mistake to assume that the resulting appearance of the world is true. Wisdom lies in the ability to look at the glasses ourselves and realize that they color our vision. Compare Beck's analogy to the following passage from Marcus Aurelius's *Meditations*:

> *The things you think about determine the quality of your mind. Your soul takes on the color of your thoughts.*
>
> MARCUS AURELIUS,
> *Meditations*, 5.16

The idea that the mind rules over everything permeates across all core Stoic teachings. It is the underlying master foundational assumption upon which the philosophy is built. Stoic philosophy claims that the path to living a good life isn't driven by "externals" such as wealth, possessions, career, or reputation. The mind rules over all, and therefore the secret to a good life is maintaining a high quality of mind.

1. *Self-sufficiency.* One of the most profound insights derived from the understanding that the mind rules everything is that we are in control of our own well-being. Most people blame their state of mind on outside influences. They believe that happiness will be found somewhere or achieved once they conquer something. But Stoicism claims that the key to happiness lies within us. It is all about our perception of things and framing of events. This insight is shared with other schools of thought. Ryan Holiday points out the similarity between this Stoic concept and a teaching from Zen Buddhism in his book *Stillness Is the Key*.

> *A student asked: "Master, where can I find Zen?"*
> *The master replied: "You are seeking for an ox while you, yourself, are on it."*
>
> ZEN BUDDHIST TEACHING,
> *Encounter Dialogues and Discourses*
> *of Baizhang Huaihai*

Seneca made a similar observation in a consolation letter to his mother, Helvia. He was exiled to the island of Corsica by the emperor Claudius in the year 41 AD. While in exile, he tried to comfort his bereaved mother.

> *It is the mind that makes us rich; this goes with us into exile. And in the wildest wilderness, having found there all that the body needs for its own sustenance, it itself overflows in the enjoyment of its own goods.*
>
> Seneca,
On Consolation to Helvia

According to Seneca, the mind is all that matters. As long as the body can satisfy its basic needs for sustenance, then the mind can find fulfillment anywhere, even in hardship, such as exile. Later in his life, Seneca would write in his *Moral Epistles* about the Greek philosopher Stilpo, a contemporary of Zeno of Citium, founder of Stoicism. Seneca praised Stilpo for his incredible ability to keep the perspective that despite losing his wife and children, he still had his mind, and therefore not all had been lost.

> *For Stilpo, after his country was captured and his children and his wife lost, as he emerged from the general desolation alone and yet happy, spoke as follows to Demetrius, called Sacker of Cities because of the destruction he brought upon them, in answer to the question whether he had lost anything: "I have all my goods with me!" [...] Those words of Stilpo's are equally those of the Stoic. He too carries his valuables intact through cities burnt to ashes, for he is contented with himself. This is the line he draws as the boundary for his happiness.*
>
> Seneca,
Moral Epistles, Letter 9

Marcus Aurelius reflected that the mind is different from anything else because it has the ability to rule itself. We control our mind, which can in turn direct itself and dictate its own experience.

> *The mind is that which is roused and directed by itself. It makes of itself what it chooses. It makes what it chooses of its own experience.*
>
> MARCUS AURELIUS,
> *Meditations*, 6.8

2. *Constant presence.* Once we understand that well-being is determined by our mind, we realize how unreasonable it is to expect that our troubles will be left behind by a change of scenery. We can run away from places and people, but we can't run away from ourselves.

> *Here is what Socrates said [...]: 'How can you wonder your travels do you no good, when you carry yourself around with you? You are saddled with the very thing that drove you away.'*
>
> SENECA,
> *Moral Epistles, Letter 28*

> *Where you arrive does not matter so much as what sort of person you are when you arrive there.*
>
> SENECA,
> *Moral Epistles, Letter 28*

> *What good does it do to you to go overseas, to move from city to city? If you really want to escape the things that harass you, what you're needing is not to be in a different place but to be a different person.*
>
> SENECA,
> *Moral Epistles, Letter 109*

A vacation can provide brief escapism, but once the initial distraction is gone, we are once again forced to face ourselves. Seneca frequently contemplates how the only real solution to our troubles is to look inward and seek an improvement of our mind through philosophy. He utilizes the analogy of a man who acquires wealth to illustrate the concept.

> *I will borrow from Epicurus: 'The acquisition of riches has been, for many men, not an end of troubles but a change of them.' I do not wonder. For the fault is not in one's wealth but in the mind itself. That which has made poverty a burden to us has made riches a burden as well. It matters little whether you lay a sick man on a bed of wood or a bed of gold; wherever he be moved, he will carry the disease with him. So, too, it matters not whether the diseased mind is set down in wealth or poverty. The malady follows the man.*
>
> Seneca,
Moral Epistles, Letter 17

We are reminded that happiness is available everywhere, as long as we have quality of mind.

> *As it is, instead of travelling you are rambling and drifting, exchanging one place for another when the thing you are looking for, the good life, is available everywhere.*
>
> Seneca,
Moral Epistles, Letter 28

The influence of the mind is poetically summarized by Publilius Syrus, a Syrian who was brought to Rome as a slave. A talented writer in Latin, one of his *sententiae* powerfully captures this Stoic lesson.

If you are to have a great kingdom, rule over yourself.

PUBLILIUS SYRUS

The solutions to our problems lie within. If you want to improve your life, first you need to improve your mind.

> *The man who has always had glazed windows to shield him from a draught, whose feet have been kept warm by hot applications renewed from time to time, whose dining halls have been tempered by hot air passing beneath the floor and circulating round the walls, - this man will run great risk if he is brushed by a gentle breeze.*
>
> Seneca,
On Providence

3. Know thyself. Perhaps the most profound use of the Wand of Hermes is to transform adversity into an opportunity for self-discovery. Adversity pushes us to the limit and allows us to learn what we're truly capable of. Zeno, founder of Stoicism, was known for claiming that "nothing is more hostile to a firm grasp on knowledge than self-deception." Seneca devotes a major section of his essay *On Providence* to reflecting on this concept of self-discovery through hardship. First, he observes that our lives are made up of both pleasant and unpleasant events. The human body responds to them differently. A life without adversities deprives us from experiencing a piece of our own nature.

> *To be always happy and to pass through life without a mental pang is to be ignorant of one half of nature.*
>
> Seneca,
On Providence

He then describes how talent is determined by the actions taken under hardship, when the stakes are the highest.

> *You learn to know a pilot in a storm, a soldier in the battle line.*
>
> Seneca,
On Providence

This logical progression results in one of my personal favorite passages in all Stoic texts. Seneca concludes that he pities the person who never experiences misfortune, since this person never has an opportunity to truly know herself.

> *You are a great man; but how do I know it if fortune gives you no opportunity to show your worth? You have entered the Olympic games, but you are the only contestant; you gain the crown, not the victory. I congratulate you not as a brave man, but as I would someone who had obtained a consulship or praetorship: "You're getting quite famous!" Likewise I might say to a good man, if no harder circumstance has given him the chance to show his strength of mind, "I judge you unfortunate because you have never lived through misfortune. You have passed through life without an opponent—no one can ever know what you are capable of, not even you."*
>
> Seneca,
On Providence

The Wand of Hermes is a powerful weapon in the Stoic Arsenal. The mental trick of transforming negative events into positives can have a considerable impact on our well-being. We cannot control what happens, but we can control how we react. An old maritime saying captures it well: we cannot control the wind, but we can direct the sail.

Lesson 14

PREMEDITATIO MALORUM

Meditate on what could go wrong.

The November 1986 issue of the *Journal of Personality and Social Psychology* included a fascinating article by psychologists Julie Norem and Nancy Cantor. The article described an experiment where individuals used a psychological strategy called "defensive pessimism" to better cope with anxiety. The strategy consisted of imagining negative future events, like something that could keep a goal from being achieved or some type of major drawback in life. By visualizing these events as if they were real possibilities, the defensive pessimist could prepare himself for potential failure and get motivated to work hard in order to avoid it. The article concluded that this mental technique could lead to higher confidence, anxiety reduction, and improved performance under stress.

1. Expect anything. This interesting experiment was a modern-day recreation of a similar Stoic exercise named *premeditatio malorum* (Latin for "premeditation of evils"). Both defensive pessimism and *premeditatio malorum* rely on prefactual thinking, or "before the fact" thinking. This denotes any cognitive strategy that involves thinking of future scenarios and imagining possible outcomes. According to the Stoic technique, we should frequently imagine what could go wrong in our lives. Seneca claims that part of the suffering caused by misfortune is due to it being unexpected. If we premeditate on the possibility of misfortune, then we take away its surprise factor, robbing it of its sting.

By looking forward to whatever can happen as though it would happen, he will soften the attacks of all ills, which bring nothing strange to those who have prepared beforehand and are expecting them; it is the unconcerned and those that expect nothing but good fortune upon whom they fall heavily.

Seneca,
On the Tranquility of the Mind

The anticipation of a negative event provides several benefits. In addition to eliminating the element of surprise, it gives us time to become psychologically prepared for it. It allows us to think about potential solutions to the problem, and maybe even avoid it. If the problem is unavoidable, we can think of ways to mitigate its impact. The key lesson is that the future is full of uncertainty, and thinking about what could go wrong is a way of reducing the suffering in case something negative does occur.

In view of this great mutability of fortune, that moves now upward, now downward, unless you consider that whatever can happen is likely to happen to you, you surrender yourself into the power of adversity, which any man can crush if he sees her first.

Seneca,
On the Tranquility of the Mind

2. *Be prepared.* Seneca made an attentive observation about misfortune. We are frequently surrounded by examples of adversity, but we rarely think about it happening to us. It does seem odd that most of us don't consider very often the possibility of bad luck coming our way despite having so many examples to pick from.

Whatever can one man befall can happen just as well to all. If a man lets this sink deep into his heart, and, when he looks upon the evils of others, of which there is a huge supply every day, remembers that they are free to come to him also, he will arm himself against them long before they attack him. It is too late to equip the soul to endure dangers after the dangers have arisen.

SENECA,
On the Tranquility of the Mind

Premeditatio malorum can be an eye-opening experience, forcing us to pay closer attention to what is happening around us. Once we realize that we aren't impervious to misfortune, and that it can happen to anyone, we become better prepared to handle it.

Many times has wailing for the dead been heard in my neighborhood; many times have the torch and the taper led untimely funerals past my threshold; often has the crash of a falling building resounded at my side; [...] Should I be surprised if the dangers that always have wandered about me should at some time reach me? The number of men that will plan a voyage without thinking of storms is very great.

SENECA,
On the Tranquility of the Mind

3. Humbleness. The realization that misfortune is common and we're all subject to it can have a humbling effect. We usually see others as being from a different group, a separate social class, or any of the many categories we create for people. But in the eyes of fate, we are all the same.

Whatever can one man befall can happen just as well to all.

SENECA,
On Consolation to Marcia

Our situation in life can change very quickly. Seneca reminds us that wealth is just a few strokes of bad luck away from poverty.

> *You say: "I did not think this could happen," and "Would you have believed that this would happen?" But why not? Where are the riches that do not have poverty and hunger and beggary following close behind?*
>
> Seneca,
On the Tranquility of the Mind

4. Upside. Arthur Schopenhauer was one of the great German philosophers of the nineteenth century. He didn't consider himself a Stoic but remarked frequently that he agreed with some core teachings from Stoicism. Schopenhauer was known as the philosopher of pessimism—unsurprising for someone who claimed that nonexistence is preferable to existence. But also unsurprising is the fact that a philosophical genius who spent decades thinking about human suffering saw great value in *premeditatio malorum*. Schopenhauer made an interesting remark about it:

> *There is use in occasionally looking upon terrible misfortunes—such as might happen to us—as though they had actually happened, for then the trivial reverses which subsequently come in reality, are much easier to bear. It is a source of consolation to look back upon those great misfortunes which never happened.*
>
> Arthur Schopenhauer,
Our Relation to Ourselves

In a rare example of seeing the cup half-full (somewhat), Schopenhauer points to the fact that most of the negative events we can imagine with *premeditatio malorum* will probably never come to pass. We should reflect on this and extract comfort from recognizing the bullets that we dodge.

Stoicism is a philosophy that demands a firm grounding in reality. We need to be realistic with ourselves and accept a harsh truth of the world: shit happens. This isn't a depressing thought—it is merely an honest observation that can help us appreciate what we have and prepare for what might come. Never let your guard down.

Lesson 15

FATE ONLY LENDS

See possessions as lent, not owned.

Few people ever lived a life so filled with accomplishments as Kublai Khan, the fifth Great Khan of the Mongol Empire. At the age of nine, his grandfather Genghis Khan already saw great potential in him and told his royal entourage: "the words of this boy Kublai are full of wisdom—pay attention, all of you." Through a combination of military and diplomatic acumen, Kublai became leader of the Mongols in 1260. He reigned over the largest contiguous empire in the history of humanity, stretching from the Pacific coast of China in the east to modern day Poland, Slovakia, and Hungary in the west. At its height, Kublai's empire controlled 16 percent of Earth's landmass and 25 percent of the world's population. He was able to achieve his grandfather's main goal—he conquered and unified all of China, which had been divided for almost four hundred years. In one of history's most fascinating anecdotes, legendary Italian explorer Marco Polo met Kublai Khan during his travels of Asia. When he returned to his native Venice, Marco Polo became known by the nickname *Milione* (which means "million" in Italian), purportedly because he frequently repeated how Kublai Khan's wealth had to be measured in millions.

Even a person like Kublai Khan, whose life may seem like a never-ending stream of successes, is subject to bad luck. Some have argued that he might actually be one of the unluckiest people in history. In the year 1274, Kublai Khan spent massive resources to create a naval fleet of over one thousand ships in an attempt to conquer Japan. The Mongolian fleet crossed the Korea Strait and was prepared to invade the Japanese island of Kyushu, when a sudden storm blowing from the east pushed the ships into rocky formations off the coast and destroyed them. Kublai Khan was completely dumbfounded by the freakish outcome. A few years later, he poured even more resources into a second invasion, this time with a fleet four times bigger. Once again the Mongol ships crossed the sea and arrived at the Japanese coast. And once again they were surprised by an unexpected typhoon, this time blowing from the west, which devastated the fleet and led to enormous casualties. These failed invasions became a major part of Japanese culture, where popular myths were created to tell the story of how the gods unleashed the *kamikaze* (Japanese for "divine wind") upon the invaders. The Mongol navy was never rebuilt again, the myth of Mongol invincibility that existed in the region was dispelled, and it is said that Kublai Khan spent the rest of his life stunned by these events.

1. *Fate only lends.* No one is impervious to the whims of fate. Kublai Khan, at the height of his power, suffered the largest and most disastrous attempt at a naval invasion in history—twice. The fickleness of fate has been a topic of human fascination (and fear) for centuries. Stoicism is filled with allusions to this topic. Epictetus famously described a clever Stoic mental trick to help us prepare for the uncertainty of the future.

> *Under no circumstances ever say "I have lost something," only "I returned it." Did a child of yours die? No, it was returned. Your wife died? No, she was returned. "My land was confiscated." No, it too was returned. "But the person who took it was a thief." Why concern yourself with the means by which the original giver effects its return? As long as he entrusts it*

> to you, look after it as something yours to enjoy only for a time—the way a traveler regards a hotel.
>
> EPICTETUS,
> *Enchiridion, Chapter 11*

Stoicism teaches that we shouldn't see our possessions as things that we own, but as things that were lent to us by nature. This teaching stems from the Trichotomy of Control. Our possessions are things that we do not control. They could be taken from us at any point, without our consent. Therefore, it is prudent to see them as temporary loans that could be called back at any time, as opposed to things to which we have perpetual proprietorship.

About 1,200 years before Kublai Khan, Seneca also experienced the capriciousness of fate. He was a sickly child born in a distant province who against all odds became a Roman senator. He was then exiled for eight years for a crime he didn't commit. During his exile, Seneca wrote a consolation letter to Marcia, a family acquaintance who mourned the death of her son. Seneca comforted her with the Stoic view of possessions as loans.

> *The properties that adorn life's stage have been lent, and must go back to their owners; some of them will be returned on the first day, others on the second, only a few will endure until the end. We have, therefore, no reason to be puffed up as if we were surrounded with the things that belong to us; we have received them merely as a loan.*
>
> SENECA,
> *On Consolation to Marcia*

Upon his return from exile, Seneca's life took another unexpected turn as he became the main advisor to emperor Nero. His position allowed him to accumulate massive influence and fortune. Later in life, Seneca tried to distance himself from Nero as the emperor developed tyrannic tendencies and displayed progressively more erratic behavior. But it was too late—Seneca was accused (almost certainly falsely) of conspiracy to kill Nero and ordered to commit suicide. Given his life experiences, it is unsurprising that Seneca put great value on the Stoic lesson about the fickleness of fate. He wrote about how viewing things as lent removes our fear from the uncertain future.

> *The wise man does not have to walk timidly and cautiously; for so great is his confidence in himself that he does not hesitate to go against Fortune, and will never retreat before her. Nor has he any reason to fear her, for he counts not merely his chattels and his possessions and his position, but even his body and his eyes and his hand and all else that makes life very dear to a man, among the things that are given on sufferance, and he lives as one who has been lent to himself and will return everything without sorrow when it is reclaimed.*
>
> SENECA,
On the Tranquility of the Mind

2. *Acceptance.* The view of our possessions as loans helps us to create detachment from them. This detachment is key to accepting losses if they occur. The term "Stoic acceptance" represents the mental ability to let things go while maintaining tranquility of mind. Certain losses are inevitable—fighting against them is futile. Sometimes we just need to return what was given to us on loan and move on.

> *When he [a wise person] is bidden to give them up, he will not quarrel with Fortune, but will say: "I give thanks for what I have possessed and held. I have managed your property to great advantage, but, since you order me, I give it up, I surrender it gratefully and gladly."*
>
> SENECA,
On the Tranquility of the Mind

Seneca's possessions were confiscated when he was sent into exile. Most people would have been devastated by this. But in a letter he wrote to his mother while in exile, Seneca displayed amazing indifference to it. He attributes his positive state of mind to the view that fortune had merely asked for him to return what she had generously given him.

> *I have accepted all the gifts of wealth, high office, and influence, which she [Fortune] has so bountifully bestowed upon me, in such a manner that she can take them back again without disturbing me: I have kept a great distance between them and myself: and therefore she has taken them, not painfully torn them away from me.*
>
> Seneca,
On Consolation to Helvia

Fate is unpredictable. We never know when she will take something away from us. But when she does, we should remember that it was fate that gave us the possession to begin with. And she gave it to us on loan. As a Swedish proverb says, "luck never gives; it only lends."

Lesson 16

SELF-DENIAL

Simulate hardship to stop fearing it.

Marcus Gavius Apicius was an extremely wealthy member of Emperor Tiberius's inner circle. A notorious gourmand, he was known for preparing grand dinner parties for the Roman elite to taste exotic dishes sourced from distant locations. He was a fan of flamingo tongue pie and recommended sauces made from silphium, a wild herb found only in distant African colonies. Apicius was so infatuated with high cuisine that once he organized a sailing expedition to the coast of Libya so that he could personally assess whether the shrimp from the region was as good as rumors claimed. After sailing about one thousand miles, he was unimpressed by what some local fisherman showed him and immediately demanded to return to Rome without ever going ashore. Such extravagant habits came with a hefty price tag. It is said that Apicius's parties and culinary endeavors reduced his fortune from 100 million to a measly 10 million sestertii. In current-day money, this would be somewhat equivalent to a billionaire being left with "only" about 100 million dollars. To Apicius, this reduction in wealth was unbearable. Afraid of living in "poverty," he committed suicide by eating a final meal drizzled with a poisonous sauce.

1. Attachments. The story of Apicius is a tragic reminder of the damage caused by unhealthy attachments. Apicius grew so attached to his life of extreme opulence that he killed himself over a fortune that most people would do anything to have. It is easy to admonish Apicius for his self-indulgence, but an honest assessment of ourselves reveals that we are oftentimes guilty of the same mistake. We grow attached to a house. To a car. To a career. And the fear of losing these things gradually becomes a source of anxiety. We lose the perspective that these things aren't truly necessary. We forget that we spent most of our lives without them, and we were perfectly fine in their absence.

Seneca's perspective on this topic was completely different from Apicius's. That's because Seneca actually lived through the experience of losing everything. He spent almost a decade exiled in the island of Corsica, living an extremely austere lifestyle. He learned how dispensable these attachments are. This experience had a profound effect on him, which he wrote about frequently.

> *Until we have begun to go without them, we fail to realize how unnecessary many things are. We've been using them not because we needed them but because we had them.*
>
> Seneca,
Moral Epistles, Letter 123

The English writer Samuel Johnson, always clever with his words, also wrote on this topic. He focused his observation on how we grow attached to unnecessary things purely because we covet what others have.

> *Many of our miseries are merely comparative: we are often made unhappy, not by the presence of any real evil, but by the absence of some fictitious good; of something which is not required by any real want of nature, which has not in itself any power of gratification, and which neither reason nor fancy would have prompted us to wish, did we not see it in the possession of others.*

Samuel Johnson,
The Adventurer, No. 111

2. Freedom. Accepting that we develop attachments to unnecessary things is one step in the right direction. But what should we do next? How can we solve this problem and separate ourselves from these unhealthy attachments? Stoicism proposes that we should engage in acts of self-denial: deliberate acts to deprive ourselves of certain pleasures.

> *Set aside now and then a number of days during which you will be content with the plainest of food, and very little of it, and with rough, coarse clothing, and will ask yourself, 'Is this what one used to dread?' It is in times of security that the spirit should be preparing itself to deal with difficult times. […] In the midst of peace the soldier carries out maneuvers.*
>
> Seneca,
> *Moral Epistles, Letter 18*

The core idea, as Seneca indicates, is that voluntary discomfort toughens us up and prepares us to deal with discomfort. Self-denial is meant to push us outside of our comfort zone and make us realize what we can endure. The real value of the exercise is entirely psychological. We suffer because we judge ourselves incapable of withstanding certain circumstances that in reality our bodies can easily tolerate. Self-denial clears up this incorrect assessment.

> *When pleasures have corrupted mind and body at once, nothing seems bearable, not because things are hard but because the person experiencing them is soft.*
>
> Seneca,
> *On Anger*

We gain freedom as we realize that our attachments aren't as necessary as we judged them to be. Seneca has wise observations on this topic. First, we must realize that if we want freedom, we need to reduce the value we give to the things we're attached to.

> *If you set a high value on liberty, you must set a low value on everything else.*
>
> Seneca,
> *Moral Epistles, Letter 104*

Then we must get used to this new reality of being dependent on fewer things.

> *Let us then get accustomed to being able to dine without the multitude, to being the slave of fewer slaves.*
>
> Seneca,
> *On the Tranquility of the Mind*

Finally, we reach a state where our dependencies are limited. We become "slaves of fewer slaves." At that point, the unpredictability of fortune is less likely to affect us.

> *We must draw in our activities to a narrow compass in order that the darts of Fortune may fall into nothingness.*
>
> Seneca,
> *On the Tranquility of the Mind*

3. *Practice.* There are different ways of practicing Stoic self-denial. Many people follow Seneca's advice and temporarily deprive themselves of certain types of foods and clothing. Others prefer cold showers or sleeping on the floor. It is important to always remember that the purpose of this exercise isn't to suffer pointlessly; it is meant to demonstrate that something considered

essential is actually expendable. In a modern context, this could mean depriving yourself from using technology for some time. Or, for an introverted person, pushing herself to participate in social situations.

The extent to which people might want to engage in self-denial depends on their personal goals and preferences. Some will benefit greatly from not drinking coffee for a day. Others might want to spend a whole month taking cold showers and eating plain food. Even the main Stoics of the Roman Empire did it in different ways. Seneca and Marcus Aurelius thought that short episodes of self-denial were sufficient to teach the lesson. Musonius Rufus, Epictetus's teacher, advocated for constant self-denial. Given his full dedication to the practice, he had interesting observations about it. In his opinion, changes to eating habits were the most challenging.

> *Although there are many pleasures which persuade human beings to do wrong and compel them to act against their own interest, the pleasure connected with food is undoubtedly the most difficult of all pleasures to combat. We encounter the other sources of pleasure less often, and we can therefore refrain from indulging in some of them for months or even years. But we will necessarily be tempted by gastronomic pleasures daily or even twice daily, inasmuch as it is impossible for a human being to live without eating.*
>
> *MUSONIUS RUFUS,*
> *Lectures included in the Anthology*
> *by Joannes Stobaeus*

He suggested a pragmatic solution to dealing with the temptation of food: choose based on nutritional content, not taste.

> *One way to become accustomed to eating a simple diet is to practice choosing food not for pleasure but for nourishment,*

not to please the palate but to strengthen the body.

Musonius Rufus,
*Lectures included in the Anthology
by Joannes Stobaeus*

Musonius applied the same pragmatism to clothing.

One should use clothing and footwear in the same way as one uses armor: to defend the body, not to show off.

Musonius Rufus,
*Lectures included in the Anthology
by Joannes Stobaeus*

The main takeaway is that self-denial teaches us about ourselves. It doesn't necessarily build resilience; it shows us the resilience we already possess but are unaware of. It frees us from attachments—and leads us closer to peace of mind.

Lesson 17

DECATASTROPHIZE

Don't add to your worries.

Albert Ellis had enormous influence over twentieth century psychology. In a 2001 issue of *Psychology Today* magazine, Robert Epstein, the magazine's editor in chief, wrote that "no individual—not even Freud himself—has had a greater impact on modern psychotherapy." Ellis first presented his ideas for rational emotive behavior therapy (REBT) at a conference of the American Psychological Association in 1956. His groundbreaking methodology for psychotherapy would eventually combine with the insights from Aaron T. Beck and evolve into the first form of cognitive behavioral therapy. Ellis published many works during his long and successful career, but arguably his most influential book was *Reason and Emotion in Psychotherapy*, published in 1962. It was in this book that Ellis coined a useful new term: *catastrophizing*.

> *Instead of becoming or remaining illogically upset over the frustrating circumstances of life, or over the real or imagined injustices of the world, a rational human being may adopt the following attitude: [...] he should perceive his own tendency to catastrophize about inevitable unfortunate situations—to tell himself: "Oh, my Lord! How terrible this situation is; I positively cannot stand it!"—and should question and challenge this catastrophizing, and*

> *change his internalized sentences to: "It's too bad that conditions are this frustrating. But they won't kill me; and I surely can stand living in this unfortunate but hardly catastrophic way."*
>
> Albert Ellis,
> *Reason and Emotion in Psychotherapy*, Chapter 3

The passage above reads like something straight out of a Stoic text. The similarity isn't mere coincidence. A few pages earlier in the book, Ellis describes where he drew inspiration for his new ideas.

> *Many of the principles incorporated in the theory of rational emotive psychotherapy are not new; some of them, in fact, were originally stated several thousand years ago, especially by the Greek and Roman Stoic philosophers.*
>
> Albert Ellis,
> *Reason and Emotion in Psychotherapy*, Chapter 2

1. *Decatastrophize.* The concept of catastrophizing—the human tendency of turning events into something bad by imposing negative value judgments—is a core Stoic notion. Stoic texts frequently mention how negative judgments are a source of avoidable suffering.

> *Don't make your ills worse for yourself and burden yourself with complaints. Pain is slight if opinion adds nothing to it. If you start to encourage yourself and say, "It's nothing, or certainly very little; let's hold out, it will soon leave off"—then in thinking it slight you will make it so.*
>
> Seneca,
> *Moral Epistles*, Letter 78

What madness it is to punish one's self for misfortune and add new ill to present ills!

Seneca,
On Consolation to Marcia

Ellis transformed Stoic teachings into a set of psychotherapeutic techniques that could be used to treat patients. One of these techniques, designed to subdue catastrophic thinking, was aptly dubbed *decatastrophizing*. According to Ellis, decatastrophizing could be directly linked to Epictetus.

> *This principle, which I have inducted from many psychotherapeutic sessions with scores of patients during the last several years, was originally discovered and stated by the ancient Stoic philosophers, especially Zeno of Citium (the founder of the school), Chrysippus, Panaetius of Rhodes (who introduced Stoicism into Rome), Cicero, Seneca, Epictetus, and Marcus Aurelius. The truths of Stoicism were perhaps best set forth by Epictetus, who in the first century AD wrote in The Enchiridion: "Men are disturbed not by things, but by the views which they take of them."*

Albert Ellis,
Reason and Emotion in Psychotherapy, Chapter 2

Decatastrophizing consists of reducing or challenging catastrophic thoughts. It is predicated on the idea that catastrophic thinking results in two main types of cognitive distortions: overestimation of how bad an event is (or can be), and underestimation of our ability to cope.

2. *Overestimation.* The most common way of catastrophizing is to exaggerate how bad something really is. We constantly create stories in our head about how an event is or will be unbearable. These stories can be filled with many types of irrational thinking:

pessimistic interpretations, unfounded claims, unrealistic assumptions, just to name a few. Seneca accurately described this type of negative mind-chatter.

> *Often when no sign indicates that anything bad is on the way, the mind makes up its own false imaginings. Either it takes some ambiguous utterance and bends it toward the worse, or it supposes that someone is more gravely offended than he really is.*
>
> Seneca,
Moral Epistles, Letter 13

There are several ways of decatastrophizing these exaggerated ideas. Let's use the following thought as an example: "My work project will fail and I'll get fired." This thought is a combination of two catastrophized hypotheses: (1) the project will be unsuccessful, and (2) the failure will result in being fired. One way of decatastrophizing this thought is to rephrase it by keeping only known facts. We don't know if the project will be successful or not—claiming that it will fail is mere speculation. There is also uncertainty about whether lack of success will lead to being fired. Therefore, the only concrete fact is that there is a project that needs to be completed. If we rephrase the thought accordingly, we're left with "I have a project due at work." Everything else is purely hypothetical pessimism. This rephrasing technique helps us separate what is objectively true from what is just gloomy conjecturing.

Psychotherapist Donald Robertson describes a second decatastrophizing technique in his book *How to Think Like a Roman Emperor*. This method, known as *objective representation*, consists of describing things in the most literal way possible. It helps us see things for what they really are, stripped from the layers of meaning and significance that we give them. Marcus Aurelius engages in this type of thinking in a passage from his *Meditations*.

Like seeing roasted meat and other dishes in front of you and suddenly realizing: This is a dead fish. A dead bird. Or that this noble vintage is grape juice, and the purple robes are sheep wool dyed with shellfish blood. [...] Perceptions like that—latching onto things and piercing through them, so we see what they really are. That's what we need to do all the time—all through our lives when things lay claim to our trust—to lay them bare and see how pointless they are, to strip away the legend that encrusts them.

MARCUS AURELIUS,
Meditations, 6.13

Through the lenses of *objective representation*, the work project is just ink printed on a piece of paper. That doesn't sound too scary. The current job is just a source of income. There are others out there. This literal description of things takes away the aura of significance and intimidation that we build around them.

Marcus Aurelius also teaches that sometimes the best solution is to just confront the feared negative outcome. What would realistically happen if the project failed and the person was fired? It wouldn't be the end of the world. The person would have to look for another job. It happens to many people every day. It might not be the most enjoyable experience, but it certainly wouldn't be unbearable. Asking "what if" questions can restore a realistic assessment of how a situation truly is. Whenever something appears to be intolerable, we should ask ourselves why we believe that's the case; chances are, we're wrong.

Don't let your imagination be crushed by life as a whole. Stick with the situation at hand and ask, "Why is this so unbearable? Why can't I endure it?" You'll be embarrassed to answer.

MARCUS AURELIUS,
Meditations, 8.36

3. Underestimation. Sometimes we catastrophize even when we maintain a fairly accurate assessment of a situation. Our mistake is that we underestimate our ability to cope with problems. Human resiliency is frequently miscalculated. Fyodor Dostoevsky wrote in *The House of the Dead* that the best definition of man is "a creature that can get accustomed to anything." I'm convinced that Seneca would agree with this definition. He wrote often about a feature of the human mind that modern psychology refers to as *emotional habituation*.

> *There is nothing for which nature deserves greater praise than this: knowing the hardships to which we were born, it invented habit as a salve to disasters; we quickly accustom ourselves to even the severest misfortunes. No one could withstand adversity if its persistence were felt with all the same force as its first blow.*
>
> SENECA,
On the Tranquility of the Mind

Suffering peaks at its onset and then gradually wears off over time. Feelings of anxiety are dampened by time and exposure to a situation. Knowledge of these mental features helps us to decatastrophize. The understanding that even the worst events can be assimilated has a therapeutic effect. Seneca expands on this idea by reminding us that everyone has something that makes them suffer. We should remember that we aren't alone with our problems. Others who have similar problems are able to overcome them. We have the potential to overcome them too.

> *Some are chained by public office, others by wealth; some carry the burden of high birth, some of low birth; some bow beneath another's empire, some beneath their own; some are kept in one place by exile, others by priesthoods. All life is a servitude. And so a man must become reconciled to his lot,*

and must lay hold of whatever good it may have; no state is so bitter that a calm mind cannot find in it some consolation.

Seneca,
On the Tranquility of the Mind

4. *Control.* Catastrophic thoughts can lead to uncontrolled emotions that hijack our mind and shut down our ability to make rational decisions. Decatastrophizing techniques are, in essence, methods of regaining control over our mind. We should strive to steer our own ships.

> *Let us steer our own ship, and not allow this power to sweep us from our course! He is a sorry steersman who lets the waves tear the helm from his hands, who has left the sails to the mercy of the winds, and abandoned the ship to the storm.*

Seneca,
On Consolation to Marcia

Decatastrophize. Don't add to your worries. Regain control.

Lesson 18

Change the Point of View

Visualize adversity from different perspectives.

───⊗∞⊗───

James Stockdale was the highest-ranking US Navy officer taken prisoner during the Vietnam War. On September 9, 1965, his Douglas A-4 Skyhawk aircraft was shot down by enemy fire while on a mission over North Vietnam. Stockdale ejected over a small village, where he was captured and taken to Hỏa Lò Prison. He spent the next eight years as a prisoner of war, subject to frequent torture, solitary confinement, and brutal psychological abuse. He was released from capture in 1973, after the United States signed the Paris Peace Accords and withdrew from the war. Stockdale was awarded the Medal of Honor in recognition of his heroic courage and resilience. Almost thirty years later, author Jim Collins interviewed Stockdale while writing a book on effective business management strategies. Collins was interested in the characteristics that made some companies great and thought Stockdale could provide valuable advice on how to overcome adversity. When asked how he was able to keep mental sanity during his years of imprisonment, Stockdale credited the Stoic texts he read in graduate school. He described his attitude toward his situation in the following way: "I never doubted not only that I would get out, but also that I would prevail in the end and turn the experience into the defining event of my life, which, in retrospect, I would not trade."

1. Storytelling. Stoicism teaches a set of mental tricks referred to as "standpoint reframing" techniques. These are techniques in which a person tries to visualize a situation through a different point of view. Jim Stockdale's description of his mindset alludes to a specific standpoint reframing technique known as *storytelling*. When a person utilizes storytelling, he thinks of how an event occurring in the present will be recounted, in the future, in the form of a story. Stockdale always kept in mind that his hardship would later be seen as a story of courage. He kept the perspective that overcoming such adversity would be a defining moment in his life, and that his story would become a motivational example. In the future, he would benefit from these stories—and so would many others. These thoughts had a psychologically alleviating effect. Seneca wrote about how keeping these future goals in mind makes current suffering more bearable.

> *True worth is eager for danger and thinks rather of its goal than of what it may have to suffer, since even what it will have to suffer is a part of its glory.*
>
> SENECA,
> *On Providence*

2. Prospective retrospection. The storytelling technique makes us jump into the future and imagine our story being told then. A related technique, *prospective retrospection*, tells us to jump into the future and imagine how the present will be remembered. Many situations that are considered difficult as they happen are later recalled as positive events.

> *And when a man is in the grip of difficulties he should say: "There may be pleasure in the memory of even these events one day."*
>
> SENECA,
> *Moral Epistles, Letter 78*

It is common for people to think fondly of the time when they were raising small children. But parents of small children know very well that the day-to-day experience can be taxing. The same is true for high school; many people recall it as a fun period in life, even though their adolescence might have been challenging. The knowledge that current circumstances will be viewed favorably in the future makes them easier to endure. As the saying goes, "someday you will miss today."

3. *Self-learned resilience*. Sometimes we forget that present events aren't as bad as events we've experienced—and overcome—before. The cumulative toll of past difficulties builds up our resilience. We should utilize these past experiences as reminders of our ability to prevail over our problems.

> *Cruel fortune bears hardest upon the inexperienced; [...] the raw soldier turns pale at the thought of a wound, but the veteran looks undaunted upon his own gore, knowing that blood has often been the price of his victory.*
>
> SENECA,
On Providence

Seneca brings up this feature of the human mind in the consolation letter he wrote to his mother Helvia from exile. He reminds her that she had lived through several misfortunes in her life—the death of her mother when she was a young child, the death of her husband, the death of a dear uncle. Someone who had overcome these traumatic events could certainly handle the exile of a son.

> *I will display before your grief all its woes and miseries: this will be to effect a cure, not by soothing measures, but by cautery and the knife. What shall I gain by this? I shall make the mind that could overcome so many sorrows, ashamed to bewail one wound more in a body so full of scars.*

> SENECA,
> *On Consolation to Helvia*

4. *Self-distancing.* The previous techniques were based on changing the point of view in regard to time. *Self-distancing* changes the point of view of the observer. It tells us to imagine how someone else would assess what is happening to us. There are events that we consider mundane when they happen to others, but we make a big deal when we are involved. Trying to visualize the event from a third-party point of view allows us to have a more down-to-earth appraisal of it.

In his phenomenal book *The Practicing Stoic*, Ward Farnsworth included a passage by Guillaume du Vair, an influential French Stoic philosopher of the Renaissance, regarding the usefulness of self-distancing.

> *Remember how you judged similar mishaps when they happened to others, and consider how you were hardly moved, and even blamed them and brushed aside their complaints… The opinions we have of another man's cause are always more just than those that we have of our own.*
>
> GUILLAUME DU VAIR,
> *The Moral Philosophy of the Stoics*

5. *Positive benchmarking.* We should also view ourselves from the point of view of others from a comparative perspective. *Positive benchmarking* is a technique where we compare ourselves to those less fortunate than us. Our current situation, as bad as it might seem, would be considered desirable by other people. A twisted ankle doesn't sound like a big problem to someone who had both legs amputated. Getting the flu is nothing for someone with incurable chronic bronchitis. Not being selected for a job promotion sounds great to the unemployed. The knowledge that we are in a better situation than others makes our suffering more manageable.

Positive benchmarking is a powerful tool when applied to people in different geographical locations or even different time periods. Some of the problems faced in rich industrialized societies seem completely trivial to those in underdeveloped countries. And we should never forget that even the kings of prior eras didn't have mundane current-day comforts such as a sewer system or refrigeration. This comparison across time was true even in ancient Rome, as Seneca describes.

> *Whenever I look back to the great examples of antiquity, I feel ashamed to seek consolation for my poverty, now that luxury has advanced so far in the present age, that the allowance of an exile is larger than the inheritance of the princes of old.*
>
> Seneca,
On Consolation to Helvia

6. *Downward counterfactual.* Stoic literature frequently mentions the capriciousness of fate. The future is full of uncertainty, and Stoicism gives us tools to mentally prepare ourselves for whatever comes our way. Given that a few twists of fate are sufficient to completely change the way an event transpires, it is helpful to think how alternative scenarios—or counterfactuals—could have been worse than the present reality. A car crash is never a pleasant experience—but someone who suffers a car accident should be grateful for still being alive to tell the story. The *downward counterfactual* mind trick can be applied to all situations since it is always possible to imagine a parallel universe where the outcome was worse. Samuel Johnson made this observation in a letter he wrote to Welsh author Hester Thrale, talking about a burglary.

> *When any calamity has been suffered, the first thing to be remembered is how much has been escaped.*
>
> Samuel Johnson,
Letter to Hester Thrale

Adversity is made more bearable when observed from different points of view. These Stoic mental tricks helped James Stockdale withstand long, dark years of enormous hardship. Most of our problems are minor when compared to his. If these techniques helped him, they can help us too.

Part 4

SYMPATHEIA

Keep reminding yourself of the way things are connected, of their relatedness. All things are implicated in one another and in sympathy with each other. This event is the consequence of some other one. Things push and pull on each other, and breathe together, and are one.

MARCUS AURELIUS,
Meditations, 6.38

Lesson 19

COSMOPOLITANISM

We are connected and depend on each other.

Michael Collins was the command module pilot of the Apollo 11 mission. He orbited the moon thirty times while Neil Armstrong and Buzz Aldrin collected rocks and performed scientific experiments on the surface. Collins didn't get the chance to walk on the moon, but he did experience more than anyone else an event that many astronauts describe as deeply profound: an earthrise. Each of the thirty orbits around the moon resulted in a clear view of Earth rising in the lunar horizon: a bright blue sphere in stark contrast against the black background of space. Collins was interviewed innumerous times about his experience after returning to Earth. When asked what stood out to him as most memorable in the mission, most people expected him to describe the mysterious features of the dark side of the moon. Instead, his response focused on Earth: "The thing that really surprised me was that it [Earth] projected an air of fragility. And why, I don't know. I don't know to this day. I had a feeling it's tiny, it's shiny, it's beautiful, it's home, and it's fragile."

Several astronauts have experienced similar thoughts. This phenomenon has been named the *overview effect*: a cognitive shift in awareness experienced by astronauts who view Earth from space. These astronauts claim that Earth looks frail and delicate from that vantage point. The view of this tiny sphere hanging in the void of space, protected by a thin atmosphere, results in a profound sense of connectedness with humanity. National borders and conflicts appear unnecessary and trivial from that perspective. These thoughts are similar to the Stoic concept of *sympatheia*—a feeling of sympathy and mutual interdependence toward others. *Sympatheia* is at the heart of Stoic ethics. It is the idea that we all share common features and depend on each other. *Sympatheia* is a key building block behind the Stoic concept of *cosmopolitanism*.

1. *Cosmopolis*. Stoicism argues that we all share a common humanity. People are born within different imaginary demarcation lines we call national borders, but we remain connected by the traits shared by our mutual nature. Early Greek philosophers would teach that their city (*polis*, in Greek) was the whole cosmos—a *cosmopolis* shared by all humans. Epictetus writes about how the concept of a "citizen of the world" dates back to Socrates.

> *The only logical step is to do as Socrates did, never replying to the question of where he was from with, "I am Athenian," or "I am from Corinth," but always, "I am a citizen of the world."*
>
> EPICTETUS,
Discourses, 1.9

The term *cosmopolitanism* describes the philosophical notions stemming out of the idea of world citizenship. Views of what cosmopolitanism entails changed over time. The cosmopolitanism of the Roman Stoics differed in some respects from that of the Greek Stoics. Seneca described the concept using the analogy of two commonwealths.

> *Let us grasp the idea that there are two commonwealths—the one, a vast and truly common state, which embraces alike gods and men, in which we look neither to this corner of the earth nor to that, but measure the bounds of our citizenship by the path of the sun; the other, the one to which we have*

> been assigned by the accident of birth. This will be the commonwealth of the Athenians or of the Carthaginians, or of any other city that belongs, not to all, but to some particular race of men. Some yield service to both commonwealths at the same time—to the greater and to the lesser—some only to the lesser, some only to the greater.
>
> SENECA,
On Leisure

According to Seneca, all humans are born with dual citizenship. The greater of those citizenships—being a cosmopolitan—is shared by everyone. The lesser one is determined by the geographical location where one is born. The cosmopolis isn't a literal location, but a conceptual interconnectedness between people. Seneca then introduces the idea of paying service to these commonwealths. Some people's actions generate a good to their nation—the lesser of the commonwealths. But some people are capable of transcending national borders and providing benefits for all of humanity. Seneca believes that Zeno and Chrysippus, early founders of Stoicism, are in this category.

> Our school [Stoicism] is ready to say that both Zeno and Chrysippus accomplished greater things than if they had led armies, held public office, and framed laws. The laws they framed were not for one state only, but for the whole human race.
>
> SENECA,
On Leisure

2. *Sympatheia.* The concept of cosmopolitanism is interesting—but what should be done about it? Unless it can be translated into action, it is just a thought experiment. This is where *sympatheia* comes into play. A feeling of connectedness with

humanity also produces empathy and compassion for others. People share the same desires and have the same fears. From an evolutionary standpoint, all humans are extremely similar. We evolved as social animals. Feeling affection for others is a trait that conferred a benefit to our ancestors, and this characteristic was passed on to everyone alive today. Some might think that living a secluded life will be beneficial for mental well-being, but people are happiest when among others. Nature made us social. *Sympatheia* is, in essence, an understanding that humans are social animals who benefit from mutual interdependence. Seneca expressed this idea eloquently.

> *Let this verse be in your heart and in your mouth: "I am a human being, I regard nothing human as foreign to me." Let us hold things in common, as we are born for the common good. Our companionship is just like an arch, which would collapse without the stones' mutual support to hold it up.*
>
> Seneca,
Moral Epistles, Letter 95

Cosmopolitanism is a method for turning *sympatheia* into action. We should feel connected to our fellow citizens of the human cosmopolis. We shouldn't confine ourselves to our corner of the globe—we should strive to reach out to others. Our nature dictates that this sociability will improve the quality of our minds.

> *The very reason for our magnanimity is not shutting ourselves up within the walls of one city, in going forth into intercourse with the whole earth, and in claiming the world as our country, was that we might have a wider field for our virtue.*
>
> Seneca,
On the Tranquility of the Mind

Seneca claims that the purpose of Stoic philosophy is to help others. To him, *sympatheia* is at the very core of what makes Stoicism worth pursuing.

> *No philosophical school is kindlier and gentler, nor more loving of humankind and more attentive to our common good [than Stoicism], to the degree that its very purpose is to be useful, bringing assistance, and consider the interests not only of itself as a school but of all people, individually and collectively.*
>
> Seneca,
On Clemency

We should always remember the human bonds that connect us. The cosmopolis depends on mutual support. If we don't help each other, the cosmopolis suffers. And when the cosmopolis suffers, we all suffer. Marcus Aurelius captured this idea in one of his most famous quotes:

> *What's bad for the hive is bad for the bee.*
>
> Marcus Aurelius,
Meditations, 6.54

Lesson 20

WE'RE MORE SIMILAR THAN DIFFERENT

Focus on similarities.

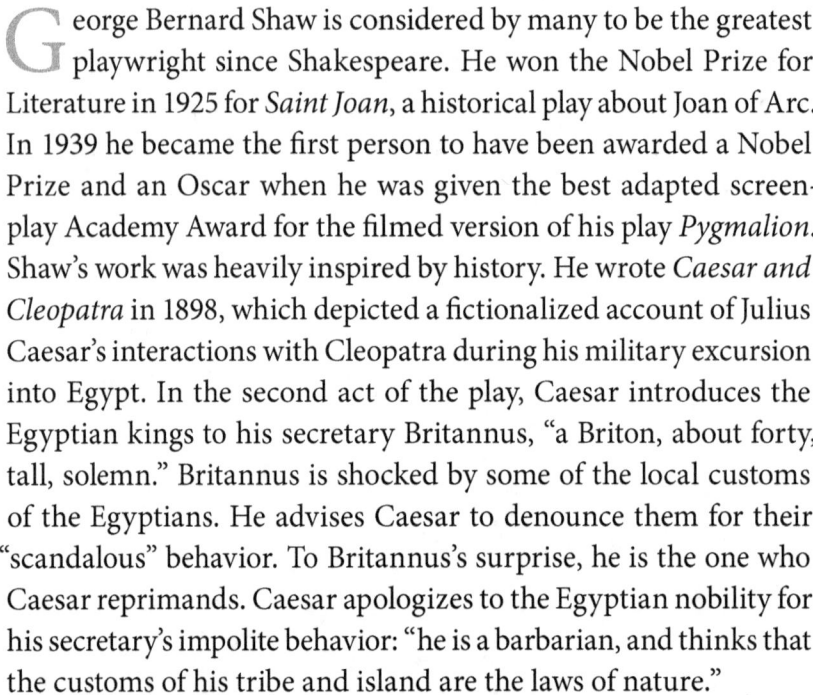

George Bernard Shaw is considered by many to be the greatest playwright since Shakespeare. He won the Nobel Prize for Literature in 1925 for *Saint Joan*, a historical play about Joan of Arc. In 1939 he became the first person to have been awarded a Nobel Prize and an Oscar when he was given the best adapted screenplay Academy Award for the filmed version of his play *Pygmalion*. Shaw's work was heavily inspired by history. He wrote *Caesar and Cleopatra* in 1898, which depicted a fictionalized account of Julius Caesar's interactions with Cleopatra during his military excursion into Egypt. In the second act of the play, Caesar introduces the Egyptian kings to his secretary Britannus, "a Briton, about forty, tall, solemn." Britannus is shocked by some of the local customs of the Egyptians. He advises Caesar to denounce them for their "scandalous" behavior. To Britannus's surprise, he is the one who Caesar reprimands. Caesar apologizes to the Egyptian nobility for his secretary's impolite behavior: "he is a barbarian, and thinks that the customs of his tribe and island are the laws of nature."

Caesar's harsh words toward Britannus are an example of Shaw's masterful writing. At first glance, it appears to be just a standard exchange where a master reprimands his subordinate. But Caesar's comment also establishes that he is a more sophisticated thinker than Britannus; he understands the differences between cultures, while his secretary has a tribal view of human diversity. The criticism that Britannus thinks his customs are the laws of nature could be applied to humanity as a whole. The human mind was evolutionarily designed to be more sensitive at spotting differences than similarities between people. We are designed to be biased toward behavior we are familiar with. This can lead to a mental blind spot, where we overemphasize differences and underestimate similarities we share with others. Shaw is very skillful in the way he alludes to this profound aspect of the human mind in such natural and unassuming dialogue.

1. Related nature. Stoicism teaches that we should fight against our natural proclivity to focus on differences. Instead, we should recalibrate our minds to scan for similarities. At the most basic level, all humans share the capacity for rational thought. Marcus Aurelius reflected on how this shared ability leads to human connectedness.

> *If thought is something we share, then so is reason—what makes us reasoning beings. If so, then the reason that tells us what to do and what not to do is also shared. And if so, we share a common law. And thus, are fellow citizens. And fellow citizens of something. And in that case, our state must be the world. What other entity could all of humanity belong to? And from it—from this state that we share—come thought and reason and law.*
>
> MARCUS AURELIUS,
> *Meditations*, 4.4

The fact that the quote above came from Marcus Aurelius makes it more fascinating. His reign as emperor of the Roman Empire was marked by wars in Mesopotamia and central Europe. He was constantly exposed to the brutal nature of armed conflict. And yet he still searched for similarities with the enemy. He never lost perspective of the humanness he shared with those at the opposite side of the battlefield.

> *I have seen the beauty of good, and the ugliness of evil, and have recognized that the wrongdoer has a nature related to my own—not the same blood or birth, but the same mind, and possessing a share of the divine.*
>
> MARCUS AURELIUS,
Meditations, 2.1

2. Golden Rule. The belief that we share similarities leads to the understanding that our preferences are also related. Therefore, the Golden Rule is evoked by several Stoic texts. Seneca brings it up when giving advice to rulers.

> *I might best set down this model for a prince to imitate: let him wish to treat his fellow-citizens as he wishes the gods to treat him.*
>
> SENECA,
On Clemency

The same advice applied to the treatment of slaves. Stoicism was one of the first schools of thought to advocate for better treatment of slaves, who made up 30 percent of the population of the Roman Empire at Seneca's time.

> *But the essence of the advice I'd like to give is this: treat your inferiors in the way in which you would like to be treated by your own superiors. And whenever it strikes you how much power you have over your slave, let it also strike you that your own master has as much power over you.*
>
> SENECA,
Moral Epistles, Letter 47

3. Ecumenism. Some of the core themes and values of Stoicism are shared with other philosophies and religions. I'm a fan of the

way in which contemporary Stoic philosopher Massimo Pigliucci phrases this idea: Stoicism is *ecumenical*—it has general application and appeal due to its contact points with other schools of thought. There are extensive studies fully devoted to outlining the similarities between Stoicism and major religions. The following passages are just a handful of examples.

Out of the main world religions, Buddhism is the one that shares the most similarities with Stoicism. Both are remarkably similar despite having been created thousands of miles apart. The various parallels stem from the fact that both advocate a search for mental well-being through introspection. The root of both philosophies is the claim that experience is dictated by the quality of the mind. One of the most fundamental Stoic teachings is that we shouldn't be attached to externals—the things we do not control. Compare that to the words of the Buddha:

> *Attachment is the root of suffering.*
>
> Siddhartha Gautama, the Buddha,
> *Majjhima Nikāya, Discourse 105*

The idea behind the Trichotomy of Control—there are things we control and things we do not—is at the heart of the Serenity Prayer. The prayer was developed by American Protestant Christian theologian Reinhold Niebuhr and is widely used in Christian evangelical worship.

> *God, grant me the serenity to accept the things I cannot change, courage to change the things I can, and wisdom to know the difference.*
>
> Reinhold Niebuhr,
> *Serenity Prayer*

The Bhagavad Gita, a section of the Hindu holy epic Mahabharata, contains several verses that are analogous to Stoic teachings. The section below, containing advice given by the god Krishna to prince Arjuna, resembles the Stoic idea of experience being driven by perception, and also the risks of being attached to externals.

> *Happiness and unhappiness are temporary experiences that rise from sense perception. Heat and cold, pleasure and pain, will come and go. They never last forever. So, do not get attached to them. We have no control over them.*
>
> Krishna,
Bhagavad Gita, 2:14

Muslim philosopher Al-Kindi wrote about how possessions should be treated as loans since they can be taken away at any time. His quote could be included in lesson 15 of this book.

> *We also should bear in mind that all that we have of common possessions is a borrowing from a lender, the Creator of the possessions, great be His praise, Who may reclaim His loan whenever He wishes and give it to anyone He wishes.*
>
> Al-Kindi,
Epistle on the Device for Dispelling Sorrows

The classic texts of Confucianism share several similarities with Stoicism. Core Confucian theory is also based on the improvement of the self through introspection. Confucius talked about his own version of *premeditatio malorum*.

> *The superior man does not forget danger in his security, nor ruin when he is well established, nor confusion when his affairs are in order. In this way he gains personal safety.*
>
> Confucius,
I Ching, Great Commentary, Sixth Wing

Stoicism teaches that we should emphasize our similarities. We are born preprogrammed by evolution to seek differences. We should take control of our minds and override this feature. We are more similar than different.

Lesson 21

FORGIVE WRONGS OF OTHERS

No one makes mistakes on purpose.

A certain Robert J. Hanlon, computer programmer from Scranton, Pennsylvania, hoped that a funny saying stuck in his head would be included in an upcoming joke book. He submitted it for consideration, and his witticism made the cut. It was published in 1980 as part of *Murphy's Law Book Two: More Reasons Why Things Go Wrong!*, the second book in the Murphy's Laws series written by Arthur Bloch. The top section of page 52 included Hanlon's submission: "never attribute to malice that which is adequately explained by stupidity." The cleverness of the saying didn't go unnoticed. Over the years it was republished by several publications. By the mid-1990s it had become popularized under the name Hanlon's Razor. In philosophy, a "razor" is a rule that simplifies a decision-making process by eliminating unlikely possibilities.

The idea behind Hanlon's Razor has been around for a long time. Goethe expressed it in his 1774 book *The Sorrows of Young Werther*:

> *Misunderstandings and lethargy perhaps produce more wrong in the world than deceit and malice do. At least the latter two are certainly rarer.*
>
> JOHANN WOLFGANG VON GOETHE,
> *The Sorrows of Young Werther*

The concept can also be traced to works by William James, Jane West, Robert Heinlein, Winston Churchill, and even Napoleon Bonaparte. It's hard to think of a better example of the randomness of jargon; a philosophical principle promoted by some of the most influential people in history ended up named after a computer programmer who wanted to tell a joke. Independent of where the name comes from, Hanlon's Razor touches upon a topic that has been a focus of philosophy for millennia: forgiveness.

1. Ignorance. Socrates was one of the first Western philosophers to ruminate on this topic. Why do people commit wrongdoings? Socrates postulated that people's actions are based on what they believe to be right. Therefore, an action is only wrong from the point of view of someone else. This insight led to one of his most famous statements:

> *No man does wrong knowingly.*
>
> SOCRATES,
> *Protagoras by Plato, 358b-c*

Socrates's words were the original version of Hanlon's Razor. The founders of Stoicism, heavily influenced by Socrates, incorporated this observation into Stoic philosophy. Around five hundred years later, Marcus Aurelius utilized this lesson to help him prepare for the challenges of everyday life.

> *When you wake up in the morning, tell yourself: The people I deal with today will be meddling, ungrateful, arrogant,*

dishonest, jealous, surly. They are like this because they can't tell good from evil.

MARCUS AURELIUS,
Meditations, 2.1

Marcus Aurelius understood that nobody is born wise. It takes a lot of time and education to develop an understanding of ethics. Most people aren't born under circumstances that allow them to go after this type of education. Their mistakes are consequences of lack of training.

> *When you have to deal with someone, ask yourself: What does he mean by good or bad? If he thinks x or y about pleasure and pain (and what produces them), about fame and disgrace, about death and life, then it shouldn't shock or surprise you when he does x or y. In fact, I'll remind myself that he has no real choice.*

MARCUS AUREALIUS,
Meditations, 8.14

Given the general lack of ethical enlightenment, we should expect to see a lot of wrong being done. The wrongdoer is unaware of the wrong he commits. We should be forgiving of mistakes caused by this widespread type of ignorance.

> *A general's strictness is unsheathed against individuals, but pardon is required when the whole army has deserted. What eliminates a wise man's anger? The great crowd of wrongdoers. He understands how unjust it is to be angry with a vice that is pandemic.*

SENECA,
On Anger

2. *Mistakes.* Some wrongs aren't committed out of ignorance but out of accidental mistakes. We should always consider this possibility and forgive these types of wrongs. Michel de Montaigne tells an interesting anecdote about how king Archelaus of Macedonia applied this concept.

> *When Archelaus, king of Macedonia, was walking along the street, someone dumped water on him. The king's attendants said that he should punish the man. "Ah, but he did not dump the water on me," the king replied, "but on the man he thought I was."*
>
> Michel de Montaigne,
Upon Some Verses of Virgil

Even the wise commit mistakes. Seneca reminds us that no one is error-proof.

> *Let's repeat to ourselves, in each man's defense, "Even the wisest men have made many a slip. No one's so circumspect that he doesn't at some point forget to be careful, no one's so experienced that something or other doesn't goad his dignity into some overheated action, no one's so fearful of giving offense that he doesn't slip into offensive behavior even as he tries to avoid it."*
>
> Seneca,
On Anger

3. *Compassion.* Stoicism does a convincing job of arguing that wrongs done out of ignorance or mistakes should be forgiven. But this is much easier said than done. The feeling of being wronged is notoriously difficult to control. Forgiveness is hard. Stoic philosophers recognized this aspect of the human mind. Epictetus proposed a counterintuitive solution: we should pity a wrongdoer.

> *(Don't be angry with wrongdoers.) Put it that way, and you'll realize how inhumane your position is. It is as if you were to say, "Shouldn't this blind man, and this deaf man, be executed?" Because if loss of the greatest asset involves the greatest harm, and someone is deprived of their moral bearings, which is the most important capacity they have—well, why add anger to their loss? If you must be affected by other people's misfortunes, show them pity instead of contempt.*
>
> Epictetus,
Discourses, 1.18

Epictetus's argument stems from the notion that mistakes are caused by ignorance. The wrongdoer is a victim of his misunderstanding about the world. We should pity and show compassion toward someone in such an undesirable position. He expands on this idea by describing how revenge is nonsensical when viewed from this point of view.

> *"Well, does that mean that if someone wrongs me I shouldn't hurt them in return?" First of all, look at what wrongdoing is and remember what you have heard about it from philosophers. Because if "good" as well as "bad" really relate to our choices, then consider whether your position does not amount to saying something like, "Well, since that guy hurt himself with the injustice he did me, shouldn't I wrong him in order to hurt myself in retaliation?"*
>
> Epictetus,
Discourses, 2.10

4. *Physician.* Seneca suggested adopting a similar perspective. If a wrongdoer suffers from something undesirable, then he should be treated in the same way that a doctor treats a patient. A physician isn't bothered by his patient's illness; he shows kindness toward him. We should adopt the same attitude toward wrongdoers.

> *What physician gets angry at a lunatic? Who takes in ill part the abuse of a man stricken with fever? The wise man's feelings towards all men is that of a physician towards his patients.*
>
> Seneca,
On the Firmness of the Wise Person

> *The wise man—calm and even-tempered in the face of error—leaves his house daily with this thought in mind: "I will encounter many people who are devoted to drink, many who are lustful, many who are ungrateful, many who are greedy, many who are driven by the demons of ambition." All such behaviors he will regard as kindly as a doctor does his own patients.*
>
> Seneca,
On Anger

5. *Self-protection.* Nero became emperor of the Roman Empire in the year 54 AD. Seneca was Nero's tutor. Within the first year of Nero's rule, Seneca wrote an essay known as *On Clemency*. The text outlined the differences between good and bad rulers. Seneca defined the term *clemency* as "the mind's moderation when it has the power to take revenge." An extensive part of the essay emphasizes that showing forgiveness toward others is more than just an act of nobility—it is an act of self-preservation. Seneca points out that clemency is like an insurance policy; we hope to never have to rely on it, but we find comfort in knowing that it is available.

> *Just as medicine has its uses among the ill but is held in honor by the healthy too, so even the innocent esteem clemency, though it's people deserving punishment who seek its support.*
>
> Seneca,
On Clemency

He also makes an observation that applies not only to rulers: those who show forgiveness garner good faith, while those who don't risk making enemies. Forgiveness is a type of self-protection.

> *Clemency not only ennobles men, it makes them safer; it is at one and the same time adornment of supreme power and its surest security. For why else do kings reach old age and bequeath their kingdoms to their sons and grandsons, while the power of tyrants is loathsome and short-lived?*
>
> Seneca,
On Clemency

The wisdom of forgiveness has been promoted for millennia. It doesn't matter if we get it from Stoicism or from a jokester computer programmer. We should remember to be less resentful and more forgiving.

Lesson 22

Focus on Virtues, Not Flaws

Emphasize positive qualities.

The year 1980 was a milestone for the Académie Française, arguably France's most famous elite cultural organization. The French Academy, as it is referred to in the English-speaking world, is the highest authority for all matters pertaining to the French language. It is composed of forty members, each one elected to a specific seat by the other members of the Académie. Voltaire held seat 33 from 1746 to 1778. Victor Hugo held seat 14 for several decades and voted to elect Alexandre Dumas for seat 2. The members are known as *les immortels* (*the immortals* in French), in allusion to their mission of forever guiding the French language. The first 661 members were all men. In 1980, Marguerite Yourcenar was selected for seat 3 and became the first woman member of the Académie. The bathroom sign at the institution's building was changed to say "Messieurs | Marguerite Yourcenar."

Yourcenar published several essays and novels during her successful career. The book that catapulted her to fame and critical acclaim was *Memoirs of Hadrian*, published in 1951. The book is written as a letter from Roman emperor Hadrian to his adoptive grandson and eventual successor, Marcus Aurelius. Yourcenar, a history enthusiast, combined factual events from Hadrian's life with fictionalized events to create a fascinating combination of biography, philosophy, meditation, and poetry. One of the themes of the book is the complexity of human character. Hadrian is depicted as wise but careless. Benevolent but at times also cruel. Yourcenar masterfully describes the multiple layers that form Hadrian's mind. The book contains rich monologues that express distinctive Stoic themes. Among the most noticeable is a Stoic teaching that was stressed in Marcus Aurelius's *Meditations*: we should focus more on people's virtues and less on their flaws.

1. Full picture. Lesson 20 of this book, titled "We're More Similar than Different," described how we are evolutionarily wired to look for differences between people, and how this can make us overlook the similarities between us. The same is also true about flaws and virtues. We tend to characterize people by what we perceive as flaws, often neglecting virtues. This propensity of the human mind can be punitive. It vastly oversimplifies the complex nature of human psychology. People are made up of multiple layers of behaviors, desires, motivations, frustrations, etc. Focusing on flaws creates an unfair assessment of the person. We should try to understand the whole picture. And once we reach a more complete understanding of the person's character, then we should strive to emphasize qualities instead of focusing on flaws. In *Memoirs of Hadrian*, this idea is articulated with eloquence:

> *Our great mistake is to try to exact from each person virtues which he does not possess, and to neglect the cultivation of those which he has.*
>
> Marguerite Yourcenar,
Memoirs of Hadrian

The excerpt from Yourcenar's novel is similar to a passage from *Meditations*:

> *When you need encouragement, think of the qualities the people around you have: this one's energy, that one's modesty, another's generosity, and so on. Nothing is as encouraging as when virtues are visibly embodied in the people around us, when we're practically showered with them. It's good to keep this in mind.*
>
> Marcus Aurelius,
Meditations, 6.48

Seneca also wrote on this topic. He makes an interesting observation: not only are we unfair by focusing on other people's flaws, but our assessment of what constitutes a flaw is oftentimes flawed. In these cases, the uncharitable view that we create of someone is not only unnecessary but also unreasonable.

> *Some men have reasons to oppose us that aren't only just but honorable. One man is looking out for his father, another for his brother, another for the fatherland, another for a friend. Yet we don't forgive these men for doing what we'd criticize them for neglecting—or rather, which is beyond belief, we often value the deed but condemn the doer.*
>
> Seneca,
On Anger

Benjamin Franklin is another thinker who wrote about this. The 1738 edition of his *Poor Richard's Almanac* contained a clever aphorism on this topic.

> *Search others for their virtues, thy self for thy vices.*
>
> Benjamin Franklin,
Poor Richard's Almanac, 1738 Edition

2. Teachers. A memorable passage from *Memoirs of Hadrian* shows an aging Hadrian reflecting on how he'd be remembered after his death. He thinks of how he viewed his predecessors as teachers. There was something to learn from all prior emperors, even the deeply flawed ones. No matter how unfavorable his opinion of these men, Hadrian could still find some virtue about them that he deemed worthy of emulating.

> *I looked for example even to those twelve Caesars so mistreated by Suetonius, the clear-sightedness of Tiberius, without his harshness; the learning of Claudius, without his weakness; Nero's taste for the arts, but stripped of all foolish vanity; the kindness of Titus, stopping short of his sentimentality; Vespasian's thrift, but not his absurd miserliness. These princes had played their part in human affairs; it devolved upon me, to choose hereafter from among their acts what should be continued, consolidating the best things, correcting the worst, until the day when other men, either more or less qualified than I, but charged with equal responsibility, would undertake to review my acts likewise.*
>
> MARGUERITE YOURCENAR,
Memoirs of Hadrian

The Hadrian created by Yourcenar is deeply wise in this regard. He recognizes that there is something to learn from all men. This concept is also found in Stoic literature.

> *You can survey everything, and because you will not find anything that as a whole you would rather be, you can pick out from each individual some traits which you would like to be given to you.*
>
> SENECA,
On Benefits

The poet Ralph Waldo Emerson summarized this idea in a timeless quote.

Every man I meet is in some way my superior; and in that I can learn of him.

RALPH WALDO EMERSON,
Think, Volume 4–5, 1938

Focusing more on virtues and less on flaws can have a profound positive effect over our mental well-being. We spend so much time ruminating on negative thoughts about other people. We can save ourselves from a lot of suffering by just accepting that people are complex and shifting the attention from flaws to virtues. It is fairer to others—and beneficial to us.

Lesson 23

IMPROVE OTHERS

When we help others, we help ourselves.

The House of Representatives Chamber in the US Capitol Building is decorated with twenty-three marble relief portraits. Each portrait depicts a historical figure who influenced the principles behind American law. The north wall of the chamber has the portrait of Lycurgus of Sparta—a fabled prince and lawmaker credited with the militaristic reformation that defined Spartan society for centuries. Epictetus used to tell a story about Lycurgus to his students—a story that was also contained in Plutarch's *Parallel Lives*. It is said that Lycurgus faced bitter backlash from Sparta's wealthy citizens when he implemented the practice of *syssitia*: obligatory common meals served at community tables for all members of society. The Spartan nobility found it demeaning to share a table with the lower classes and organized a protest against it. Lycurgus was attacked by a mob and blinded in one eye by a young man named Alcander. The revolt was contained by royal guards before more damage could be done. Alcander was handed over to Lycurgus to punish as he saw fit. Instead of treating the young man with harshness, Lycurgus gave him a complete education and turned him into a respectable citizen. Once the training was complete, Lycurgus introduced Alcander publicly at a full theater. Many of Lycurgus's followers were indignant, accusing him of not punishing the young man sufficiently. To those criticisms, Lycurgus replied: "The person you gave me was violent and aggressive; I'm returning him to you civilized and refined."

1. Education. The story about Lycurgus's treatment of Alcander lies at the heart of a key Stoic teaching: seek to improve others. This idea is linked to the Stoic concept of *sympatheia*. The social nature of humans makes us empathetic. Helping others to improve their lives improves our own mental well-being. It also has more practical ramifications since the ones we improve share society with us; by improving them, we improve our own living conditions. The best way of improving someone is by providing education. Knowledge has a transformational effect that cannot be matched by anything else. Lycurgus was aware of this when shaping his treatment of Alcander. Epictetus talked about the importance of learning and tied it to the idea that "no one makes mistakes on purpose," as mentioned in lesson 21.

> *My judgement is poor and I don't know what I really should be doing. But if this can neither be learned nor taught, then don't blame me for it. If it can, however, then either teach it to me yourself, or let me learn from someone who professes to know; since I hope you don't suppose that if I'm doing the wrong thing it's by choice. So what else could explain my error but ignorance? And wouldn't you rather I be cured of that?*
>
> EPICTETUS,
> *Discourses, 1.26*

Marcus Aurelius held a strict view on this matter. He held himself accountable for teaching others. If he didn't, then he considered their future mistakes to be his own fault.

> *If they've made a mistake, correct them gently and show them where they went wrong. If you can't do that, then the blame lies with you. Or no one.*
>
> MARCUS AURELIUS,
> *Meditations, 10.4*

2. *Kindness.* Educating others is difficult. The wrongdoer is unaware of his mistakes. He will deem education unnecessary. He will fight against change. So how should we go about it? Marcus Aurelius stresses that kindness is key.

> *Kindness is invincible, provided it's sincere—not ironic or an act. What can even the most vicious person do if you keep treating him with kindness and gently set him straight—if you get the chance—correcting him cheerfully at the exact moment that he's trying to do you harm. [...] Don't do it sardonically or meanly, but affectionately—with no hatred in your heart.*
>
> Marcus Aurelius,
Meditations, 11.18.9

Seneca echoed similar sentiments. We should help others with honesty and respect. His advice calls for *sympatheia*: we should invoke our feelings of mutual relatedness toward others.

> *[The wise man] will bring succor to another's tears, not join in them; he will give a hand to the shipwrecked, shelter to the exile, a coin to the needy—not the insulting sort of offering that most of those who want to appear compassionate just toss away, disgusted by those they help and afraid of being touched by them, but a coin given by one human being to another from a source they share.*
>
> Seneca,
On Clemency

3. *Self-control.* Anger is a common reaction to other peoples' mistakes. Our evolutionary wiring makes us feel satisfaction when we reprimand someone. But this type of reaction is counterproductive. There is truth to the common saying "lose your temper, lose the argument." Epictetus talked about how anger makes matters worse.

> *When did anger ever teach someone to play music or pilot a ship? Do you imagine that your anger is going to help teach me the far more complex business of life?*
>
> Epictetus,
> *Discourses, 1.26*

Marcus Aurelius also advised against reacting angrily to people's mistakes. He analyzed the situation from an interesting perspective.

> *How cruel—to forbid people to want what they think is good for them. And yet that's just what you won't let them do when you get angry at their misbehavior. They're drawn toward what they think is good for them. "But it's not good for them." Then show them that. Prove it to them. Instead of losing your temper.*
>
> Marcus Aurelius,
> *Meditations, 6.27*

This is a fascinating observation because it is so obvious and yet a perspective rarely taken. People do what they think is right. If we get angry at their behavior, then they will think that we are trying to keep them from doing what is good for them. As Marcus Aurelius points out, this is a cruel thing to do. The goal is to be perceived as a benevolent teacher, not an oppressor. The appropriate course of action is to exert self-control and explain the position in a compassionate way.

4. *Role model.* Lycurgus was successful in transforming Alcander because he embodied what he taught. Alcander had an example to emulate. One of the most efficient ways of improving others is to teach by example. People respond positively to those who show kindness and empathy toward them. They gradually take on those characteristics themselves. Musonius Rufus challenged his students to respond to wrongs by being models of civility.

> *It is characteristic of a civilized and humane temperament not to respond to wrongs as a beast would and not to be implacable towards those who offend, but to provide them with a model of decent behavior.*
>
> Musonius Rufus,
> Lectures included in the Anthology
> by Joannes Stobaeus

Donald Robertson tells an interesting story about Marcus Aurelius in *How to Think Like a Roman Emperor*. During his youth, Marcus Aurelius had a grammar instructor named Alexander of Cotiaeum. The instructor made a lifelong impression on Marcus Aurelius because of the tactful way in which he corrected people's grammatical mistakes. Alexander didn't explicitly point out a mistake; he knew how to discretely guide the person in the right direction. Even decades later, Marcus Aurelius wrote about it in *Meditations*.

> *On Alexander of Cotiaeum: Not to be constantly correcting people, and in particular not to jump on them whenever they make an error of usage or a grammatical mistake or mispronounce something, but just answer their question or add another example, or debate the issue itself (not their phrasing), or make some other contribution to the discussion—and insert the right expression, unobtrusively.*
>
> Marcus Aurelius,
> Meditations, 1.10

Improving others requires kindness. It requires self-control. It requires being our best selves and teaching by example. But the payoff is certainly worth it. Stoicism teaches a clear lesson: by improving others, we improve ourselves.

Lesson 24

SHOW APPRECIATION

Give and receive appreciation considerately.

Seneca's longest work dealing with a single subject was a series of seven books focused on an unexpected topic. The books, dedicated to Seneca's close friend Aebutius Liberalis, are known today as *On Benefits*. In the original Latin, the work is entitled *De Beneficiis*. The word *beneficiis* (plural form of *beneficium*) doesn't have an exact translation in English. It means a favor, appreciation, gift, or any act of kindness in general. Seneca's translation indicates the complexity of the term.

> *So what is a beneficium? It is a well-intentioned action that confers joy and in so doing derives joy, inclined towards and willingly prepared for doing what it does. And so it matters not what is done or what is given, but with what attitude, since the benefit consists not in what is done or given but rather in the intention of the giver or agent.*
>
> SENECA,
> *On Benefits*, Book 1

The English word *benefits* doesn't capture the full meaning of the original. Some scholars have suggested that *On Kind Deeds* would be a more faithful title. Translation arguments aside, many are surprised that Seneca would devote so much time and effort to writing a heptalogy on a subject that might sound somewhat inconsequential to modern audiences. But in ancient Rome, demonstrations of appreciation were far from trivial; they were a crucial element of social stability. One of the most striking statistics about the Roman Empire is that 20 percent of its emperors were assassinated while in power. Being emperor in ancient Rome had a fatality rate equivalent to unvaccinated and untreated typhoid fever. Assassinations among senators and other members of the political class were also common. Exchanges of kind deeds were a way of signaling good will that could reduce the chances of violence. Far from superficial, it was a necessary component of social cohesion.

Much of the art of showing appreciation has been lost over time. Modern societies are formed by more stable institutions and therefore require fewer displays of sympathy to maintain social order. But the Stoic lessons on this topic are still very relevant. They form an important component of *sympatheia*, leading to an increased sense of mutual connectedness and empathy among people. According to Seneca, the effective exchange of *beneficiis* requires some rules of engagement. Those who are giving the benefit (showing their appreciation) follow one set of rules, while those who are receiving the benefit (being appreciated) follow a different code of civility.

1. Giving. The person who gives a benefit is, by definition, the one who initiates the exchange. Being in this starting position requires careful consideration of certain aspects. The mode and tone in which the deed is given will dictate the manner in which it will be received and reciprocated. According to Seneca, the first rule of giving is a modified version of the Golden Rule: give in the way you would want to receive. The purpose of showing appreciation is to confer joy to someone else. No one likes to receive a compliment that is given reluctantly or in bad manner. If the benefit isn't perceived as something positive, then the exchange fails its goal.

Can anyone be grateful to a person who arrogantly tosses off the benefit, angrily throws it in his face, or gives it only out of weariness, to avoid further hassle? It is a big mistake to suppose that the recipient will reciprocate when you have worn him out with delays and tortured him with uncertainty. A benefit is owed with the same attitude as that which it is given; that is why it should not be given carelessly.

SENECA,
On Benefits, Book 1

The giver should also remember that the exchange is meant to be relational and not transactional. Both parties should feel like the display of appreciation enhances their bond. A kind deed that is performed with the intention of benefiting the giver is a business transaction, not a display of appreciation.

If you are planning to give it [a benefit], then you will give it in the way that does most good for the recipient. You will be satisfied to be your own witness in the manner. Otherwise, the satisfaction doesn't come from granting the benefit but from being seen to have done it.

SENECA,
On Benefits, Book 2

Seneca tells an anecdote about a man who gave a loan to a friend and then walked around town boasting about his generosity. Bothered by the self-aggrandizing behavior, the friend assumed that the loan had already been repaid.

The giver of a benefit should be silent; the recipient should do the talking. Otherwise, the donor will be told the same thing as was said to the man who constantly boasted of having conferred a benefit on someone. His recipient said,

> "Surely you won't deny that you've been repaid?" When the man responded, "When?" he said, "Quite often and all over the place—whenever and wherever you told people about it."
>
> Seneca,
On Benefits, Book 2

The act of showing kindness toward someone else forms a deep memory that we carry for forever. Studies with older adults suffering from memory loss indicate that memories of helping others are some of the most enduring. Seneca makes this observation and points out that the giving of a benefit can never be taken away.

> *The things we hold in our hands, which we gaze upon, the things that are the focus of our desires, these things are vulnerable; bad luck and injustice can take them away from us. But a benefit endures even when we have lost the thing through which it was given; for the benefit is a virtuous act, and no violence can nullify it.*
>
> Seneca,
On Benefits, Book 1

2. *Receiving.* The etiquette around receiving a benefit is centered around demonstrating gratitude. As explained in the prior section, the main purpose of the person giving appreciation is to confer joy to the one receiving it. Therefore, responding to a kind deed with gratitude is crucial for the exchange to be successful.

> *What is the intention of the person who gives a benefit? To be useful to the recipient and to give him pleasure. If he achieved this objective and if his intention got through to me and we felt mutual pleasure, then he got what he was aiming at. For*

> he did not want to be given something in exchange; otherwise it was not a benefit but a business deal.
>
> SENECA,
> On Benefits, Book 2

A common mistake people make is to think that displays of appreciation should be reciprocated with an equivalent display of appreciation. A gift for a gift. A benefit for a benefit. But this view falls for the trap of interpreting the exchange as transactional. The true repayment for a benefit is a demonstration of sincere gratitude.

> Receiving a benefit with gratitude is the first installment of its repayment.
>
> SENECA,
> On Benefits, Book 2

Cicero, considered by many to be Rome's greatest orator, shared Seneca's view of the importance of demonstrating gratitude. In his seminal speech *Pro Plancio*, he argued that gratitude was the parent of all other virtues.

> While I wish to be adorned with every virtue, yet there is nothing which I can esteem more highly than being and appearing grateful. For this one virtue is not only the greatest, but is also the parent of all the other virtues.
>
> CICERO,
> *Pro Plancio*

Seneca also stressed that we shouldn't evaluate a benefit based on its size or extravagance, but on the means and intent of the giver. A small heartfelt gift is always superior to a big one given with indifference.

What this person gave to me was very small; but he could do no more. What this person gave is great; but he was hesitant, he put it off, he moaned while he was giving, he gave arrogantly, and he paraded the fact that he was giving, and did not intend to give pleasure to the recipient. He gave to his own ambition and not to me.

Seneca,
On Benefits, Book 1

The final advice on receiving benefits is to never forget about them. The hedonic treadmill can make us desire new things and forget about what was given to us in the past. A person who demonstrated kindness toward us ends up being forgotten as we switch focus to a new desire.

When the desire for novelties makes what you have been given seem unimportant, the donor comes to be underappreciated. We loved and admired someone and admitted that he was the basis for our current prosperity—but only so long as we were pleased by what we got from him.

Seneca,
On Benefits, Book 3

This type of ingratitude is a shameful faux pax in the world of exchanging benefits. Seneca talks about how we often act in this inconsiderate manner toward our teachers.

So it happens that our teachers and the benefits they conferred on us are forgotten, because we have left our entire childhood behind; and so it happens that we lose sight of what was done for us in our adolescence, because we never look back at that stage of our life. All of us treat prior events not as things in the past, but as things that have passed away.

Seneca,
On Benefits, Book 3

A demonstration of appreciation is an effective way of bonding. Given our social nature, bonding experiences have a positive impact over our mental well-being. We should put more effort into practicing this ancient technique for building meaningful relationships.

Lesson 25

Character Is All That Matters

Judge others based exclusively on their character.

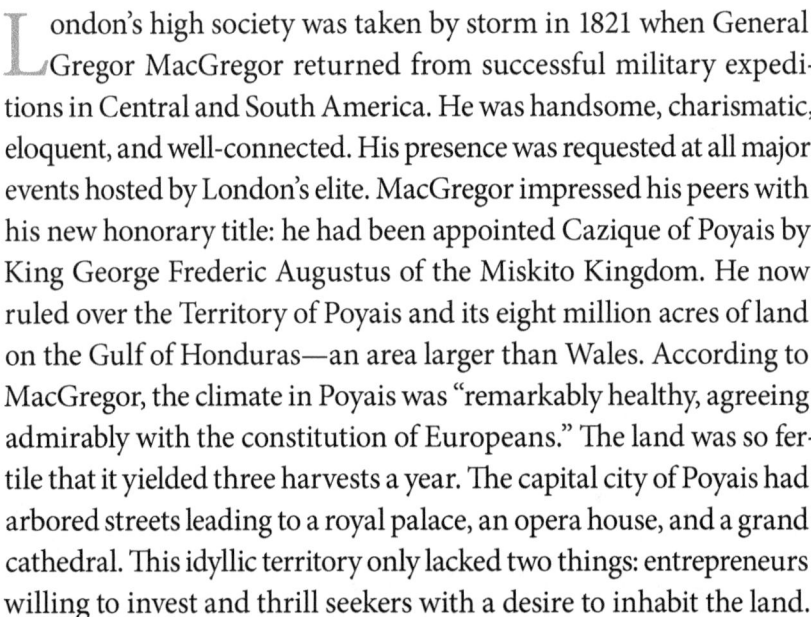

London's high society was taken by storm in 1821 when General Gregor MacGregor returned from successful military expeditions in Central and South America. He was handsome, charismatic, eloquent, and well-connected. His presence was requested at all major events hosted by London's elite. MacGregor impressed his peers with his new honorary title: he had been appointed Cazique of Poyais by King George Frederic Augustus of the Miskito Kingdom. He now ruled over the Territory of Poyais and its eight million acres of land on the Gulf of Honduras—an area larger than Wales. According to MacGregor, the climate in Poyais was "remarkably healthy, agreeing admirably with the constitution of Europeans." The land was so fertile that it yielded three harvests a year. The capital city of Poyais had arbored streets leading to a royal palace, an opera house, and a grand cathedral. This idyllic territory only lacked two things: entrepreneurs willing to invest and thrill seekers with a desire to inhabit the land.

MacGregor found both within a few months. He raised considerable capital when the London Stock Exchange listed bonds denominated by the Government of Poyais. Several investors purchased Poyaisian land certificates, and around three hundred Londoners signed up to settle the land. The captivating new kingdom of Poyais and its charming leader were the talk of the town. Unfortunately, it was all a lie. MacGregor is known today as one of the greatest con artists in history. Poyais was just a swampy, inhospitable bay on the coast of present-day Nicaragua. The Miskito, an indigenous group, found no use for the hostile land and gladly traded it to MacGregor in exchange for some rum and jewelry. The three hundred settlers arrived upon two sail ships and were shocked by the uncharted jungle. Soon they faced starvation, malaria, and yellow fever. Less than fifty of them made it back to London. MacGregor ran away from England and tried running a similar fraud scheme in France, where he was caught and accused of charlatanism. He escaped prosecution by fleeing to Venezuela, where he lived the rest of his days.

1. *Mind over matter.* The story of Gregor MacGregor's fantastical scam illustrates how easily the human mind can be fooled by appearances. A sweet-talking con artist got the London Stock Exchange to issue bonds of a country that didn't even exist. His sophisticated finesse convinced three hundred people to give up their life savings and travel across the Atlantic to a fictitious land. MacGregor's claims were full of inconsistencies. How come no one had ever heard of this new country? Who was this mysterious King George Frederic Augustus of the Miskito Kingdom? Why was MacGregor given full autonomy over such prime land? It would've taken just some minor research to uncover the fraud. But people were so captivated by his charm that they forgot to put any due diligence into his real character. Stoic philosophers were aware of this type of human gullibility. Seneca had several observations on this topic. He drew a comparison with buying a horse to point out the foolishness of judging people based on appearances.

> *A man who examines the saddle and bridle and not the animal itself when he is out to buy a horse is a fool; similarly, only an absolute fool values a man according to his clothes, or according to his social position, which after all is only something that we wear like clothing.*
>
> SENECA,
> *Moral Epistles, Letter 47*

Seneca was especially critical of venerating people because of their wealth and fame. Despite being wealthy and famous himself, he understood that those things could be achieved by people of deeply flawed character. In his opinion, we commit the mistake of being influenced by one's notoriety when assessing their true character.

> *None of those who have been raised to a lofty height by riches and honors is really great. Why then does he seem great? Because you are measuring the pedestal along with the man. A dwarf is not tall, though he stands on a mountain; a Colossus will maintain its size even when standing in a well. This is the error under which we labor, and how we are deceived; we value no man by what he is, but add the trappings in which he is adorned.*
>
> SENECA,
Moral Epistles, Letter 76

We should value others based on the quality of their minds. Fame, fortune, and appearance are descriptive characteristics about them that don't tell us much about their true character. What truly matters cannot be seen from the outside.

> *Your merits should not be outward facing.*
>
> SENECA,
Moral Epistles, Letter 7

2. Praiseworthiness. Stoic philosophers noticed an interesting inconsistency in human behavior. The story of Gregor MacGregor is infuriating not only because of his fabrications, but also because of the naiveté of the people who fell for them. We are critical of others who do not value people correctly. But when it comes to ourselves, we are perfectly fine with being valued too highly and receiving undeserved praise. We are honored when someone gives us undue compliments and then admonish that same person for glorifying a phony celebrity. We should strive for honest assessments. Part of the problem is that we feel pride for things that aren't truly ours. We believe that the things we possess should somehow translate into positive assessments of ourselves. Seneca points out how we shouldn't seek praise for what isn't ours.

> *In a man praise is due only to what is his very own. Suppose he has a beautiful home and a handsome collection of servants, a lot of land under cultivation and a lot of money out at interest; not one of those things can be said to be in him—they are just things around him. Praise in him what can neither be given nor snatched away, what is peculiarly a man's.*
>
> SENECA,
> *Moral Epistles*, Letter 41

Epictetus made the same observation using the example of a horse.

> *Don't pride yourself on any assets but your own. We could put up with a horse if it bragged of its beauty. But don't you see that when you boast of having a beautiful horse, you are taking credit for the horse's traits? What quality belongs to you?*
>
> EPICTETUS,
> *Enchiridion*, Chapter 6

We shouldn't take credit for our possessions, and we shouldn't praise others for their possessions. The emphasis should be on a person's character, not on what he owns.

> *Anyone entering our homes should admire us rather than our furnishings.*
>
> SENECA,
> *Moral Epistles*, Letter 5

3. *Virtue*. The concept of judging others based exclusively on character is harder than it sounds. Even when we filter out fame and possessions, it can still be hard to assess someone's true character. Stoicism gives us helpful advice: focus on actions. Character is revealed more by actions than by words. Those who act with virtue are worthy of praise, and virtue can be displayed by anyone, independent of status.

> *Virtue shuts the door on no one. It is open to everyone and lets us all in, invites us in: the freeborn, ex-slaves, slaves, kings, and exiles. It does not choose ancestry or wealth; virtue is satisfied with the bare person.*
>
> Seneca,
On Benefits, Book 3

Seneca tied this concept to the Stoic idea of cosmopolitanism. According to him, we are all part of the same cosmopolis, and the only thing that differentiates us one from another is the virtue we express.

> *We are all made of the same elements and we all have the same origin. No one is more noble than anyone else, except the person with a character that is more upright and equipped with more good traits. There are people who display ancestral masks in their foyers and post their long and intricate family tree right at the entrances of their palatial homes—but are they not notorious rather than noble? The cosmos is the sole parent of us all, and everyone's ancestry is traced back to that source, whether the pathways to that origin are glorious or humble.*
>
> Seneca,
On Benefits, Book 3

Stoicism reminds us that character is all that matters. We should judge others based on the virtue they display in their actions. Appearances can be deceiving, and therefore shouldn't be included in the assessment of one's character. The poet Ralph Waldo Emerson, strongly influenced by Stoicism, summarized this lesson with eloquence:

> *The essence of greatness is the perception that virtue is enough.*
>
> Ralph Waldo Emerson,
Essays: First Series, Heroism

Part 5

PRAGMATISM

*On my adoptive father, Antoninus Pius:
The way he handled the material comforts that
fortune had supplied him in such abundance—without
arrogance and without apology. If they were there,
he took advantage of them. If not, he didn't miss them.
The way he looked to what needed doing and not
the credit to be gained from doing it.*

MARCUS AURELIUS,
Meditations, 1.16

Lesson 26

STOP COMPLAINING

Respond to challenges with pragmatism.

Frederick the Great, King of Prussia from 1740 to 1786, always carried books about Stoicism with him. When asked the reason behind the habit, he replied: "Stoicism sustains you in misfortune." This response highlights a key reason why the philosophy of Stoicism is so attractive: it is useful. Stoicism, especially the one practiced by the Roman Stoics, differentiates itself from other schools of philosophy in the emphasis it gives to providing practical advice. Frederick the Great wasn't looking for an epistemological discussion on whether self-justified basic positions of knowledge are logically sound. He needed advice on how to tame anxiety before a battle. He wanted to know how to live a better life while ruling a complex kingdom. In summary: he needed realistic, practical, effective advice that could be immediately applied to his life. Stoicism excels beautifully in providing this type of pragmatic guidance.

The no-nonsense attitude that defines Stoicism is vividly displayed in an interaction between Musonius Rufus and Demetrius the Cynic, documented in Philostratus's *Life of Apollonius of Tyana*. Musonius was sent into exile by Emperor Nero in the year 65 AD. He was sent to Greece and forced to work on the Isthmus of Corinth, an artificial canal that would provide a shortcut connecting the Ionian and Aegean seas. Demetrius, an antagonist of Musonius, was traveling through the area and saw Musonius digging with a pickax under the scorching summer sun. Demetrius couldn't resist the urge to provoke his old foe. He stopped by to greet Musonius and ask if he was enjoying his new line of work. Musonius replied with the typical Stoic matter-of-factness: "Do I upset you, Demetrius, to be digging the isthmus for Greece? I wonder what you would have thought if you saw me playing the lyre like Nero."

1. Pragmatism. Looking at things with pragmatism is at the heart of Stoicism. A Stoic knows how to decatastrophize. He keeps a cosmic perspective. He knows what he controls and what he doesn't control. Musonius Rufus knew what his punishment entailed. From a practical standpoint, he was just working on a construction project that would benefit Greece. That was more noble than sitting in a palace playing the lyre. Complaining wouldn't change anything, so he accepted his fate and moved on, without making a big deal. Marcus Aurelius valued this type of no-nonsense attitude.

> *Everything that happens is either endurable or not. If it's endurable, then endure it. Stop complaining. If it's unendurable, then stop complaining. Your destruction will mean its end as well. Just remember you can endure anything your mind can make endurable, by treating it as in your interest to do so.*
>
> Marcus Aurelius,
Meditations, 10.3

Seneca also advocated for the same pragmatism. He tied it to the Stoic teaching that things aren't good or bad, but our judgments make them so. The things we complain about are only worthy of complaints because we make them out to be. This is especially true for things that happened in the past. What is the practical purpose of being unhappy today over what happened yesterday?

A man is as unhappy as he has convinced himself he is. And complaining about one's suffering after they are over [...] is something I think should be banned. Even if all this is true, it is past history. What's the good of dragging up sufferings which are over, of being unhappy now just because you were then?

SENECA,
Moral Epistles, Letter 78

2. Keep moving. Stoicism teaches that we shouldn't allow externals to interfere with our objectives. We should keep moving toward our goals no matter what obstacles appear in the way. Marcus Aurelius described this state of mind in one of his most recognized lessons.

The mind adapts and converts to its own purposes the obstacle to our acting. The impediment to action advances action. What stands in the way becomes the way.

MARCUS AURELIUS,
Meditations, 5.20

The idea that "impediment to action advances action" is a powerful reminder of the importance of framing. Some people respond to an obstacle with complaints and demotivation. But we can choose to utilize the Wand of Hermes and perceive the obstacle as an opportunity to improve ourselves and get closer to reaching a goal. The obstacle becomes a catalyst for action, and what was once impeding our path becomes part of the path. Marcus Aurelius frequently mentioned the importance of maintaining this type of attitude.

The cucumber is bitter? Then throw it out. There are brambles in the path? Then go around them. That's all you need to know. Nothing more. Don't demand to know "why such things exist." Anyone who understands the world will laugh at you, just as a carpenter would if you seemed shocked at finding sawdust in his workshop, or a shoemaker at scraps of leather left over from work.

MARCUS AURELIUS,
Meditations, 8.50

3. *Expectations.* Frustrated expectations are a common cause for complaining. As Stoicism teaches, our expectations are fully within our control. The easiest way to solve this problem is by developing a habit of setting more realistic expectations. Marcus Aurelius wrote about how we are often surprised—and made upset—by things that should've been expected.

> *Remember: you shouldn't be surprised that a fig tree produces figs, nor the world what it produces. A good doctor isn't surprised when his patients have fevers, or a helmsman when the wind blows against him.*
>
>
>
> MARCUS AURELIUS,
> *Meditations, 8.15*
>
>

A Stoic sets expectations so as not to be frustrated by events. The ability to effectively handle a wide range of experiences is the mark of a healthy mind.

> *A healthy pair of eyes should see everything that can be seen and not say, "No! Too bright!" A healthy sense of hearing or smell should be prepared for any sound or scent; a healthy stomach should have the same reaction to all foods, as a mill to what it grinds. So too a healthy mind should be prepared for anything. The one that keeps saying, "Are my children all right?" or "Everyone must approve of me" is like eyes that can only stand pale colors, or teeth that can handle only mush.*
>
>
>
> MARCUS AURELIUS,
> *Meditations, 10.35*
>
>

It is unrealistic to expect a world where everyone behaves virtuously all the time. We should always be prepared to run into people behaving unethically. That's the reality of the world—complaining has no effect over it. We can only accept it and adapt our expectations accordingly.

> *When you run up against someone else's shamelessness, ask yourself this: is a world without shamelessness possible? No. Then don't ask the impossible. There have to be shameless people in the world. This is one of them. The same for someone vicious or untrustworthy, or with any other defect.*
>
> MARCUS AURELIUS,
> *Meditations, 9.42*

We can use this Stoic lesson on a daily basis, every morning when we wake up. Marcus Aurelius reminded himself to not complain about the day ahead.

> *At dawn, when you have trouble getting out of bed, tell yourself: "I have to go to work—as a human being. What do I have to complain of, if I'm going to do what I was born for—the things I was brought into the world to do? Or is this what I was created for? To huddle under the blankets and stay warm?"*
>
> MARCUS AURELIUS,
> *Meditations, 5.1*

Stoicism provides us with an abundance of techniques on how to respond to adversity. Complaining is not one of them. We should handle life's challenges with pragmatism and move on.

Lesson 27

DON'T SEEK RECOGNITION

Seek being worthy of recognition.

Confucius lived in the State of Lu, China. His philosophy—Confucianism—was a major influence in the shaping of virtually all East Asian cultures, most notably in China, Japan, and Korea. Without a doubt, he was one of the most influential individuals in human history. Around one hundred fifty years before Zeno founded Stoicism, Confucius already lectured his followers on some topics that, to modern-day audiences, sound very Stoic. Lesson 20 talked about how Stoicism is an ecumenical philosophy. Confucianism was mentioned as one of the philosophical traditions with which it shares contact points. The similarities with the teachings of Confucius are particularly striking in the topic of not being allured by recognition.

1. Virtue. According to Confucius, wisdom lies in the understanding that recognition isn't something we should seek. Our goal should be to act with virtue, in a way that a wise person would find praiseworthy. The recognition itself is just a potential side consequence of virtuous actions. This teaching is summarized in the fourth book of Confucius's *Analects*.

> *I am not concerned that I am not recognized, I seek to be worthy of being recognized.*
>
> CONFUCIUS,
Analects, Book 4

Roughly seven hundred years later and six thousand miles away, Marcus Aurelius echoed the same sentiments in his *Meditations*.

> *Beautiful things of any kind are beautiful in themselves and sufficient to themselves. Praise is extraneous. The object of praise remains what it was—no better and no worse. [...] Does anything genuinely beautiful need any supplementing? Are any of those improved by being praised? Or damaged by contempt? Is an emerald suddenly flawed if no one admires it?*
>
> MARCUS AURELIUS,
> *Meditations,* 4.20

The belief that recognition shouldn't be sought, but considered a potential by-product of virtuous action, is infused throughout Stoic literature. Epictetus taught his students that they shouldn't seek praise for their philosophical erudition. Instead, they should demonstrate their knowledge through action.

> *Sheep don't bring their owners grass to prove to them how much they've eaten, they digest it inwardly and outwardly bring forth milk and wool. So don't make a show of your philosophical learning to an uninitiated, show them by your actions what you have absorbed.*
>
> EPICTETUS,
> *Enchiridion, Chapter 46*

Seneca focused on how the reward for a virtuous act is the act itself. Recognition is completely unnecessary.

> *"What shall I gain," someone may say, "if I do this with courage, if I do this with gratitude?" Your gain will be that you have done it—nothing more is promised you. The reward for*

honorable actions lies in the actions themselves.

SENECA,
On Benefits, Book 4

2. **Sympatheia.** Helping others is one of the ultimate Stoic goals. Human nature dictates that we are social animals, and we are evolutionarily wired to feel satisfaction when we help others. Some people forget about this aspect of human nature. They believe that a charitable act needs to be repaid with praise. Stoicism teaches that benevolence is rewarding in and of itself. We should act charitably without the desire or expectation of being lauded for it.

> *What else did you expect from helping someone out? [...] As if your eyes expected a reward for seeing, or your feet for walking. That's what they were made for. By doing what they were designed to do, they're performing their function. Whereas humans were made to help others. And when we do help others—or help them to do something—we're doing what we were designed for. We perform our function.*
>
>
>
> MARCUS AURELIUS,
> *Meditations, 9.42*
>
>

To further this point, Marcus Aurelius noted an interesting way in which humans behave differently from animals and other things in nature.

> *Some people, when they do someone a favor, are always looking for a chance to call it in. And some aren't, but they're still aware of it—still regard it as debt. But others don't even do that. They're like a vine that produces grapes without looking for anything in return. A horse at the end of the race. A dog when the hunt is over. A bee with its honey stored. And a human being after helping others. They don't make a fuss*

> *about it. They just go on to something else, as the vine looks forward to bearing fruit again in season.*
>
> MARCUS AURELIUS,
Meditations, 5.6

He advises us to do what is right without any considerations for whether we'll be given any credit for it. The real world isn't like the utopian city of Kallipolis that Plato describes in his *Republic*. The real world is complex and full of flaws; all we can do is act with virtue.

> *Set yourself in motion—if you have it in you—and don't worry whether anyone will give you credit for it. And don't go expecting Plato's Republic; be satisfied with even the smallest progress, and treat the outcome of it all as unimportant.*
>
> MARCUS AURELIUS,
Meditations, 9.29

3. **Madness.** Stoic literature calls attention to a foolish type of thought that many of us are guilty of having. We often seek the recognition of people whose values we disagree with. People admire the things that they value. Therefore, the only way we will gain admiration from those with different values is if we change our values to match theirs. It sounds insane to seek success according to other peoples' definition of success—especially if their definition is at odds with ours. In this case, we should be more than happy to forgo their recognition.

> *Who are these people whose admiration you seek? Aren't they the ones you are used to describing as mad? Well, then, is that what you want—to be admired by lunatics?*
>
> EPICTETUS,
Discourses, 1.21

> *How foolish one must be to leave a lecture hall gratified by the applause of the ignorant! Why do you take pleasure in praise from those you cannot praise yourself?*
>
> Seneca,
Moral Epistles, Letter 52

The pursuit of recognition is a flawed endeavor. We should act based on what is virtuous, not on what we believe will result in the most praise. Virtuous action is a reward on its own; recognition is unnecessary. Confucius agreed with this core Stoic lesson.

> *The wise man is distressed if he acts unvirtuously. It is no trouble to him if he is not recognized by others.*
>
> Confucius,
Analects, Book 15

Lesson 28

DON'T SEEK HAPPINESS

Happiness is a by-product of virtue.

John Stuart Mill is considered the most influential English language philosopher of the nineteenth century. A precocious child, he learned Greek at the age of three, mastered math, physics, and astronomy at eight, and had already read several classical works of philosophy at ten. At fifteen, economist David Ricardo would invite him to his house to debate about political economy. Mill went on to develop a unique style of philosophy that combined ideas from eighteenth century Enlightenment with new nineteenth century currents of thought. He gave special emphasis to individual liberty and independence from governmental oversight. Later in his life, he became a Member of Parliament and was a pioneer in the fight for women's rights in Britain. Mill didn't consider himself a Stoic philosopher, but throughout his career he voiced several times his affinity for some of the key Stoic teachings. His 1859 philosophical essay *On Liberty* displayed his thoughts about Marcus Aurelius:

> *If ever anyone, possessed of power, had grounds for thinking himself the best and most enlightened among his contemporaries, it was the Emperor Marcus Aurelius. Absolute monarch of the whole civilized world, he preserved through life not only the most unblemished justice, but what was less*

> *to be expected from his Stoical breeding, the tenderest heart. [...] His writings [were the] highest ethical product of the ancient mind.*
>
> JOHN STUART MILL,
> *On Liberty*, Chapter 2

Mill's areas of philosophical focus changed throughout his career. His last book published in life was his *Autobiography*, in which he dedicated an extensive section to reflect on the pursuit of happiness. This was a topic over which Mill had ruminated extensively—he struggled for many years with a depression so severe that he was incapable of writing. These dark times led him to a counterintuitive realization: the secret to finding happiness is to not seek for it.

1. *En passant*. John Stuart Mill believed that happiness can only be achieved through an indirect approach. Happiness, according to him, is a by-product of acting with virtue. We experience happiness when we help others or when we make a positive impact in the world. Happiness isn't the objective we seek, but it comes along *en passant*.

> *Those only are happy who have their minds fixed on some object other than their own happiness; on the happiness of others, on the improvement of mankind, even on some art or pursuit, followed not as a means, but as itself an ideal end. Aiming thus at something else, they find happiness by the way. The enjoyments of life are sufficient to make it a pleasant thing, when they are taken en passant, without being made a principal object.*
>
> JOHN STUART MILL,
> *Autobiography*, Chapter 5

Now compare Mill's words to a passage from Seneca's essay *On the Happy Life*:

> *As in a plowed field, which has been broken up for corn, some flowers will spring up here and there, yet it was not for these little plants, although they may please the eye, that so much toil was expended—the sower had a different purpose, these were superadded—just so happiness is neither the cause nor the reward of virtue, but its by-product, and we do not accept virtue because she delights us, but if we accept her, she also delights us.*
>
> SENECA,
> On the Happy Life

Seneca was a strong proponent of the idea that happiness is only achieved indirectly. He mentions it various times across his writings. In Letter 27 of his *Moral Epistles*, Seneca urges his friend Lucilius to give up his vices. Seneca explains that vices might bring short-term happiness but lead to suffering in the long term. The only way of achieving lasting happiness is to have a good character, act virtuously, and enjoy happiness as a side consequence.

> *A good character is the only guarantee of everlasting, carefree happiness. Even if some obstacle to this comes on the scene, its appearance is only to be compared to that of clouds which drift in front of the sun without ever defeating its light.*
>
> SENECA,
> Moral Epistles, Letter 27

Contemporary psychologists have endorsed the Stoic view of happiness. Psychotherapist Viktor Frankl, founder of logotherapy, endorses this view of happiness in his book *Man's Search for Meaning*, where he chronicles his experiences as a prisoner in a Nazi concentration camp.

Don't aim at success. The more you aim at it and make it a target, the more you are going to miss it. For success, like happiness, cannot be pursued; it must ensue, and it only does so as the unintended side effect of one's personal dedication to a cause greater than oneself or as the by-product of one's surrender to a person other than oneself. Happiness must happen, and the same holds for success: you have to let it happen by not caring about it.

VIKTOR FRANKL,
Man's Search for Meaning

The American Psychological Association publishes the journal *Emotion*, containing significant contributions to the study of human emotions. The August 2011 edition had the results of a study entitled "Can Seeking Happiness Make People Happy? Paradoxical Effects of Valuing Happiness." A team of psychologists concluded that people who focused on searching for happiness ended up less happy. The researchers included the following statement in their final deliberations: "it may be advantageous to encourage people to follow John Stuart Mill's suggestion not to have their mind fixed on their personal happiness."

2. *Eudaimonia*. The topic of pursuit of happiness raises an important question: what is the definition of *happiness*? Stoic happiness is defined by the concept of *eudaimonia*. As mentioned in the Introduction of this book, *eudaimonia* can be translated into "well-being" or "life-satisfaction." It is also a synonym for "living a good life." This definition of happiness has a direct consequence on the path recommended to achieve it. *Eudaimonia* can't be reached through a quick thrill; it is a fully encompassing notion, and therefore requires a deeper experience. Stoicism teaches that we feel a strong bond to other humans due to *sympatheia*, and this can be the key to finding true happiness.

True happiness lies in granting well-being to many.

SENECA,
On Clemency

John Stuart Mill reached the same conclusion.

> *All those to whom I looked up, were of opinion that the pleasure of sympathy with human beings, and the feelings which made the good of others, and especially of mankind on a large scale, the object of existence, were the greatest and surest sources of happiness. Of the truth of this I was convinced.*
>
> JOHN STUART MILL,
Autobiography, Chapter 5

Seneca described how happiness is attained by helping others, even if the process of providing help is arduous. This observation leads to a surprising conclusion: happiness can be a by-product of a burdensome experience.

> *Our idea of happiness is to confer benefits even if they involve effort, provided that they reduce the efforts of others; even if they involve danger, provided they rescue others from danger; even if they strain our finances, provided they relieve the wants and hardships of others.*
>
> SENECA,
On Benefits, Book 4

In the end, those who have the wisdom to act with virtue are the ones who attain *eudaimonia*.

> *Here is the result of wisdom: a constant and unvarying kind of joy. The mind of the wise man is like the heavens beyond the moon: the sky up there is always clear… This joy is produced only by a consciousness of the virtues.*
>
> SENECA,
Moral Epistles, Letter 59

The Stoic advice to achieve happiness might seem counterintuitive, but the idea that we should aim for virtue and catch happiness as a side-effect has been validated throughout history. Modern psychology indicates that it is effective. The greatest philosopher of his generation reached the same conclusion.

> *Ask yourself if you are happy, and you cease to be so. The only chance is to treat, not happiness, but some end external to it, as the purpose of life.*
>
> John Stuart Mill,
Autobiography, Chapter 5

Lesson 29

Choose Friends Wisely

Be careful who you associate with.

July 3, 1582, was marked by a great loss to humanity. It was the day on which James "The Admirable" Crichton was murdered in the city of Mantua, Italy. He was only twenty-one years old. In his short life, he had already accomplished so much that he was compared to Leonardo da Vinci. Crichton was born in the small settlement of Clunie, Scotland. An enormously gifted prodigy from an early age, he graduated from the University of St Andrews at the age of fourteen with bachelor's and master's degrees. He was a polymath who excelled in languages, arts, and sciences. He was also a skilled horseman, fencer, and musician, and admired for his good looks and refined social skills. Such an impressive range of talents earned him the nickname "The Admirable." His fame was solidified after an event in which he challenged professors from the Collège de Navarre in France to debate him in any subject, practical or theoretical, in any of the twelve languages he spoke. All professors who took on the challenge were outclassed by his knowledge.

Crichton traveled across France and Italy, participating in academic debates and producing works in literature, music, and mathematics. In 1581 he arrived at Mantua, hired by the Duke of Mantua to be a part of the royal council. It is at this point of his life that things started taking a negative turn. Crichton developed a friendship with the Duke's son, prince Vincenzo Gonzaga. The prince was known around town as spoiled, entitled, and prone to erratic behavior. He was a regular at Mantua's bars and brothels, usually accompanied by a group of equally unruly friends. Crichton gradually became a part of Gonzaga's gang. He started frequenting lowly places and forming relationships with dubious characters. The influence of this new group of friends led Crichton to make several bad decisions. The worst one was convincing Gonzaga's mistress to take him as her new lover. Gonzaga was infuriated. On the night of July 3rd, Crichton was ambushed by a group of masked men. The leader of the group revealed himself to be Vincenzo Gonzaga. He stabbed Crichton with a sword, killing him instantly. Just like that, "The Admirable" was gone. One of the most promising geniuses in history lost his life at only twenty-one years of age because of bad associations.

1. Influence. Stoicism has a lot to say about choosing who we associate with. We are social animals that feel *sympatheia*. Achieving *eudaimonia* depends on our relationships with others. Therefore, establishing positive friendships is key to our pursuit of mental well-being. The central Stoic claim about friendship is that our friends will influence us. No one is fully impervious to the influence of those he interacts with. Epictetus voices this idea very explicitly.

> *If a companion is dirty, his friends cannot help but get a little dirty too, no matter how clean they started out.*
>
> EPICTETUS,
Enchiridion, Chapter 33

If we know our companions are going to influence us, then we need to select them wisely. Someone will start exerting influence over you the moment he is added to your circle of associations. Seneca describes a constructive friendship as one of mutual improvement. We should associate with people who have qualities we value and would like to cultivate in ourselves.

Associate with people that are likely to improve you. The process is a mutual one: men learn as they teach.

Seneca,
Moral Epistles, Letter 7

There are certain qualities that we should deliberately look for in those we choose to associate with. Seneca believes that calm personalities are especially helpful to interact with.

Our intimates should be very calm and easy to get along with, not nervous and cross-grained. We pick up habits from our companions, and just as some disorders are transmitted by bodily contact, so the mind passes on its defects to those closest at hand. [...] Minds wanting in strength profit from keeping company with a better crowd.

Seneca,
On Anger

Epictetus makes a thought-provoking observation about how we interact with friends from the past. Stoicism teaches that the acquisition of wisdom is a lifelong journey (more of this in lesson 35). We should never stop trying to improve ourselves. This perpetual self-improvement process makes us change throughout our lives. The person we are today might be quite different from the person we were in the past. Unfortunately, some of our associations might not understand or support our growth. They might want to change us back to the way we were before or treat us differently because of it. Epictetus cautions about not falling for this type of peer pressure.

You should be especially careful when associating with one of your former friends or acquaintances not to sink to their level; otherwise you will lose yourself. If you are troubled by the idea that "He'll think I'm boring and won't treat me the way he used to," remember that everything comes at a price. It isn't possible to change your behavior and still be the same person you were before.

Epictetus,
Discourses, 4.2

2. *Trust.* Friendship depends on trust. A true friendship is based on *sympatheia*—it is marked by a mutual desire for the other one's well-being. Someone who exclusively seeks his own interests in a friendship isn't a true friend.

> *Anyone thinking of his own interests and seeking out friendship with this in view is making a great mistake. Things will end as they began; he has secured a friend who is going to come to his aid if captivity threatens: at the first clank of a chain that friend will disappear. These are what are commonly called fair-weather friendships. A person adopted as a friend for the sake of his usefulness will be cultivated only for so long as he is useful. [...] The ending inevitably matches the beginning: a person who starts being friends with you because it pays him will similarly cease to be friends because it pays him to do so.*

Seneca,
Moral Epistles, Letter 9

Several of Seneca's works alert against the dangers of insincere friendships. This is unsurprising given that Seneca spent decades involved with the politics of the Roman Empire, notorious for its backstabbing. He commented on how flattery and envy usually come side by side.

> *To know how many are jealous of you, count your admirers.*

Seneca,
On the Happy Life

According to Seneca, the only way of protecting ourselves against people with secondary intentions is to perform the necessary due diligence before we engage in friendship.

> *Certainly you should discuss everything with a friend; but before you do so, discuss in your mind the man himself. After friendship is formed you must trust, but before that you must judge. Those people who judge a man after they have made him their friend instead of the other way round, certainly put the cart before the horse. Think for a long time whether or not you should admit a given person to your friendship. But when you have decided to do so, welcome him heart and soul, and speak as unreservedly with him as you would with yourself.*
>
> SENECA,
Moral Epistles, Letter 3

True friendships are rare. That's why they're so valuable. A good friend can have a lasting, positive impact in our lives. The tragic story of James "The Admirable" Crichton shows us what associating with the wrong people can do. Stoicism instructs us to be careful when choosing who we associate with. Those who are lucky to have true friendships hold an immensely valuable asset.

> *You do not know how great is the value of friendship if you do not understand that you will be giving someone a great deal by giving him a friend, something rare not only in palaces but in centuries, nowhere more lacking than where it is thought to abound.*
>
> SENECA,
On Benefits, Book 6

Lesson 30

Have a Sense of Humor

Respond to adversity with humor.

Seneca produced an eclectic body of work. He wrote several philosophical essays and nine tragic dramas. Up until the sixteenth century, it was commonly believed that Seneca the philosopher and Seneca the dramatist were two different people; it seemed unlikely that the same person could be so talented in such different genres. Among his extensive list of works, there is one that isn't mentioned very often. The name of this work already indicates that it is different from the rest: *The Pumpkinification of Claudius the God*. It is a satire on the Roman emperor Claudius, written after the emperor's death. Claudius had exiled Seneca to the island of Corsica for almost one decade—undoubtedly a motivating factor for Seneca to mock him. The plot begins with Claudius arriving in heaven after his death. The Roman gods soon realize that he doesn't belong there and send him to the underworld, where he is sentenced to spend eternity as a menial law clerk (an allusion to Claudius's nonsensical interferences with the Roman judicial system). Seneca starts the satire with a poetic description of Claudius's last moments:

> *His last words heard among mortals—after he had let out a louder sound from that part with which he found it easier to*

communicate—were as follows: "Good heavens. I think I've shat myself." Well, I don't know about that, but he certainly shat up everything else.

SENECA,
The Pumpkinification of Claudius the God

It is unexpected to read poop and fart jokes in something written by Seneca. But his more popular philosophical texts are filled with passages that show he had a sense of humor. Seneca wrote regularly about how humor is a necessary piece of well-being. Findings from modern psychology corroborate with him. Studies show that a good sense of humor is a sign of psychological health. Clinical psychologists Herbert M. Lefcourt and Rod A. Martin wrote about this in *Humor and Life Stress: Antidote to Adversity*, published in 1986:

A central thesis of this book is that humor and laughter represent an important mechanism for coping with many of the psychosocial stressors that humans encounter in their daily lives. Thus, it is our contention that humor and laughter play an important role in the maintenance of both psychological and physiological health and well-being in the face of stress.

H. M. LEFCOURT AND R. A. MARTIN,
Humor and Life Stress: Antidote to Adversity, Chapter 1

1. Rose-tinted glasses. Lesson 1 mentioned Aaron T. Beck's analogy of color-tinted glasses. According to Beck, our mental state is a consequence of the way we perceive things around us—a lesson at the core of Stoic philosophy. We can choose to look at an event through sad, blue-tinted glasses or happy, rose-tinted ones. The event itself is outside of our control and will remain objectively unchanged either way, but we have full control over how we perceive it. Maintaining a sense of humor is an inclination toward favoring the rose-tinted glasses over the blue ones.

> *Interpreting certain things a certain way makes them look like injuries. The proper course is to defer some things, laugh off others, and forgive still others. Anger should be hedged about in various ways; most things should be turned into a joke. When Socrates was struck on the head, he made no response save to say that it was a bother people didn't know when it was a good idea to wear a helmet when leaving the house.*
>
> Seneca,
On Anger

Seneca's claim that "most things should be turned into a joke" can be easily misinterpreted. It doesn't mean that we should treat things with derision. It also doesn't mean that we should adopt a "fake-happy" attitude toward life. The key idea is that living life with blue-tinted glasses will lead to unnecessary suffering. We should wear the rose-colored glasses more often and take things lightly with more frequency. Many of the problems we face aren't as important or as serious as we make them out to be. Turning them into a joke is a way of alleviating stress.

Seneca used a comparison between Democritus and Heraclitus to illustrate this point. Both were geniuses of philosophy whose contributions impacted the history of the Western world. Democritus was known as the "laughing philosopher" because of the emphasis he placed on humor throughout his life. Heraclitus, on the other hand, was considered a misanthrope by his peers and became known as the "weeping philosopher." Both were admired for their intellect, but only Democritus was seen as an example of a life worth emulating.

> *We ought, therefore, to bring ourselves to believe that all the vices of the crowd are, not hateful, but ridiculous, and to imitate Democritus rather than Heraclitus. For the latter, whenever he went forth into public, used to weep, the former to laugh; to the one all human doings seemed to be miseries,*

to the other follies. And so we ought to adopt a lighter view of things, and put up with them in an indulgent spirit; it is more human to laugh at life than to lament over it.

SENECA,
On the Tranquility of the Mind

2. Connectedness. Shared humor is a key component of social bonding. Social relationships are strengthened when people laugh together. Stoicism emphasizes how human connectedness is important for positive mental health. Having a sense of humor is an opportunity to build camaraderie, and, consequently, improve our minds. An anecdote about Antigonus, king of Macedonia after the death of Alexander the Great, illustrates how a sense of humor can help build trust.

> *Take Antigonus: nothing would have been easier for him than to order the execution of the two common soldiers who, while leaning against his tent, were expressing a low opinion of their king. Antigonus heard everything, since only a curtain separated the speakers and their audience: lightly drawing the curtain aside, he said, "Go a bit farther off, so the king doesn't hear you."*

SENECA,
On Anger

The troops under Antigonus's command became more loyal to him after hearing about his sense of humor and lighthearted treatment of the two soldiers. Similarly, Cato won the graces of the Roman Senate by his use of humor in an incident that involved Lentulus, a notorious curmudgeon.

> *When Cato was arguing a case, the notorious Lentulus—a wild, divisive statesman in our fathers' lifetime—spat squarely*

in his face. Cato wiped his face and said, "I'll bear witness to all, Lentulus, that those who say you have no talent are dead wrong."

SENECA,
On Anger

3. Encouragement. Humor has an unparalleled ability to make light of a difficult situation. It is especially powerful when a person going through hardship uses it to comfort those around him. Not everyone is a Stoic. We can learn Stoicism and develop the mental ability to effectively deal with adversity, but we do not control how those around us face adversity. Many Stoics have noted that when faced with a negative event—diagnosis of a terminal disease, for example—they were able to handle it effectively, but were upset by how it could cause suffering to their loved ones. This is where humor can have a positive impact on those around us. A sense of humor in difficult situations shows that we aren't affected by the circumstances—and signals to our loved ones that they shouldn't be either. Julius Canus, a Stoic philosopher condemned to death by emperor Caligula, was playing a game of chess with a friend when he was made aware of the sentence. He had the mental firmness to use humor in response to the news.

> *[Julius Canus] was playing chess when the centurion who was dragging off a whole company of victims to death ordered that he also be summoned. Having been called, he counted the pawns and said to his partner: "See that after my death you do not claim falsely that you won," then nodding to the centurion, he said: "You will bear witness that I am one pawn ahead."*

SENECA,
On the Tranquility of the Mind

The story of Julius Canus's death also tells that he kept his sense of humor as the execution approached. He reminded his friends that he would be the first among them to solve a mystery.

> *His [Julius Canus's] friends were sad at the thought of losing such a man; but "Why," said he, "are you sorrowful? You are wondering whether our souls are immortal; but I shall soon know."*
>
> SENECA,
On the Tranquility of the Mind

Seneca himself employed this use of humor when condemned to death by Nero. Tacitus, considered by modern scholars to be one of the greatest Roman historians, wrote about Seneca's death in his *Annals*. According to Tacitus's recount, Seneca was unmoved when told about his death sentence. His family was visibly upset, but he mocked the situation: "Was the cruelty of Nero unknown to any of us?"

4. *Self-defense.* Modern day politicians frequently stoop to low levels when attacking their adversaries. But even the dirtiest attacks we see today are tame compared to what happened in the Roman Senate. A fascinating study by Professor Martin Jehne from the Dresden University of Technology listed some of the most common attacks made by Roman senators. Turns out that Roman politicians frequently called each other *exoltus* (Roman slang for male prostitute) and threatened their adversaries with *irrumatio* (oral rape). Only the thick-skinned survived in this ruthless environment. Seneca believed that the best antidote against verbal abuse was self-deprecation.

> *No one becomes a laughingstock who laughs at himself.*
>
> SENECA,
On the Tranquility of the Mind

People who can laugh at themselves carry a valuable skill. Self-deprecation is a well-tested countermeasure against personal attacks. Modern psychological studies indicate that a person who can laugh at himself is perceived as being more approachable and relatable. It signals that the person is confident enough to admit to shortcomings, a trait that correlates highly with effective leadership. Overall, it indicates that a person has external self-awareness: the ability to accurately understand how he is viewed by others. Seneca recommended a matter-of-fact response toward insults. We should assess whether there is any truth to what is said. If yes, then it isn't an insult, but an honest remark.

> *One can say to himself [regarding insults]: "Do I, or do I not, deserve these things? If I do deserve them, there is no insult—it is justice; if I do not deserve them, he who does the injustice is the one to blush."*
>
> SENECA,
On the Firmness of the Wise Person

> *Some jest at the baldness of my head, the weakness of my eyes, the thinness of my legs, my build. But why is it an insult to be told what is self-evident? [...] Just as if these would become more notorious by another's imitating them than by our doing them!*
>
> SENECA,
On the Tranquility of the Mind

5. *Defiance.* Stoic philosophers have a long history of using humor as an act of defiance. Joking amidst a high-stakes situation is the ultimate demonstration of indifference toward externals.

> *A tyrant was threatening the philosopher Theodorus with death and even with lack of burial. [...] He [Theorodus]*

replied: "You are a fool if you think it makes any difference to me whether I rot above ground or beneath it."

SENECA,
On the Tranquility of the Mind

I have to die. If it is now, well then I'll die now; if later, then now I will take my lunch, since the hour for lunch has arrived—and dying I will tend to later.

EPICTETUS,
Discourses, 1.1

Humor is an effective way of alleviating stress and anxiety. It is helpful not only for the person with a sense of humor, but also for those around him. Lord Byron summarized it well: "Always laugh when you can; it is cheap medicine."

Lesson 31

Control Your Anger

Anger is like a madness; it should be controlled and purged.

Cyrus the Great invaded Babylon in the year 539 BC. The conquest solidified Cyrus's control of the region and turned the First Persian Empire into the largest empire the world had seen to that point. An interesting event took place in the buildup to the invasion. Cyrus, marching with his army toward Babylon, reached the banks of the Diyala River (known at the time as the Gyndes). As they prepared to cross, one of the horses that customarily pulled Cyrus's chariot was swept away by the current and drowned. Cyrus was incensed. He cursed profusely at the river. He promised the gods that he would weaken it so much that women would be able to cross it without even getting their knees wet.

Cyrus placed the march to Babylon on hold and ordered his best engineers to come up with a way of reducing the intensity of the river's flow. The Persian army was put to work digging an extensive network of 180 channels connected to 360 streams that dispersed the water of the river's main bed. By the end of the project, Cyrus's army crossed the river by foot. But it took them the whole summer, utilized massive resources, and made the siege of Babylon a much more difficult task than it would've been otherwise.

1. Madness. Seneca included this anecdote about Cyrus in his essay *On Anger*. Most of Seneca's philosophical works covered multiple topics, but *On Anger* was devoted exclusively to this one emotion. Seneca considered anger to be the most dangerous of all emotions. He compared it to a type of madness, capable of making a brilliant leader like Cyrus waste a whole summer with a nonsensical construction project to enact revenge on a river.

> *Some wise men have said that anger is a brief madness: for it's no less lacking in self-control, forgetful of decency, unmindful of personal ties, unrelentingly intent on its goal, shut off from rational deliberation, stirred for no substantial reason, unsuited to discerning what's fair and true, just like a collapsing building that's reduced to rubble even as it crushes what it falls upon.*
>
> SENECA,
On Anger

This madness can be so extreme that even the most loved ones can become a target of the angry.

> *Angry people curse their children with death, themselves with poverty, their households with ruin, and they deny they're angry just as madmen deny they're insane. They're enemies to their closest friends, people to be shunned by their nearest and dearest.*
>
> SENECA,
On Anger

Seneca wasn't the only Stoic philosopher to write about anger. Marcus Aurelius also noted the derangement caused by it. He commented on how angry actions are worse than their cause.

> *How much more damage anger and grief do than the things that cause them.*
>
> MARCUS AURELIUS,
Meditations, 11.18.8

Anger is dangerous. The manner in which we act while angry can be extremely destructive to ourselves. What should we do about it? How can we avoid the unnecessary self-inflicted suffering caused by anger? Seneca thought that our primary goal should be to avoid getting angry. But if we are overtaken by anger, then we should go into damage-control mode and avoid doing wrong.

> *As I see it, there are two main aims: that we not fall into anger, and that we not do wrong while angry.*
>
> Seneca,
On Anger

2. Control. How can we avoid getting angry? The advice makes sense, but it is certainly much easier said than done. Seneca understood how difficult it is to control anger. Most of his essay *On Anger* is a collection of mental techniques that help pacify our senses when we feel anger starting to form. Seneca's starting observation is that acting in anger is controllable. The initial anger we feel toward something is a natural impulse, such as fright or disgust. But to act in anger requires more than just that. It requires a rational deliberation to do so. Seneca described the series of events that lead to an anger-based action.

> *Anger ventures nothing on its own but acts only with the mind's approval: for (a) having the impression that one has been done a wrong, (b) desiring to take vengeance for it, and then (c) combining both in the judgment that one ought not to have been harmed and that one ought to be avenged—none of this is proper to a mere impulse set in motion independent of our will.*
>
> Seneca,
On Anger

The first takeaway is that the progression described by Seneca can be interrupted before it runs to completion. The rational parts of our brain have time to interfere with the sequence before we act out of anger. We just need mental techniques that are effective at not letting anger consume us.

3. *Judge fairly.* One of these techniques is the deliberate attempt to judge the situation impartially. Seneca says that whenever we feel anger starting to form, we should force ourselves to act like a judge. It is a mental game where we are given the task of impersonating a judge. How would an impartial arbitrator analyze the situation? Implementing this heuristic can help to placate our anger.

> *Let's reflect that even those who act willingly and knowingly don't have the wrong itself as their aim in wronging us: either the person slipped in offering some urbane pleasantry, or he did not to vex us but because he couldn't achieve his goal without getting us out of the way. Often flattery, while trying to charm, gives offense. Anyone who recalls how often he's been falsely suspected, how many of his own appropriate actions bad luck has made look like wrongs, how many people he came to like after hating them will be able to avoid becoming angry instantly, at least if he says to himself, each time he's offended, "I myself have made this mistake too."*
>
> SENECA,
On Anger

This exercise highlights situations in which we are being hypocritical. We are often angered by actions that we frequently take ourselves. This realization can also have a moderating effect over anger.

> *Suppose you're told that someone has spoken ill of you. Consider whether you did it first; consider how many you badmouth. I stress this point: let's reflect that some aren't doing us a wrong but are returning one.*
>
> SENECA,
On Anger

> *No one says to himself, "This thing that's making me angry—either I've done it myself, or I could have."*
>
> SENECA,
On Anger

4. **Clemency.** Lesson 21 holds the key to an effective anger-management strategy. *Clemency*, defined as "the mind's moderation when it has the power to take revenge," is a noble attitude to have toward others. We should train ourselves to perceive clemency as an indispensable trait. If we are successful at elevating the virtue of clemency to a high enough status, then our minds are likely to recall it in times of anger.

> *It's the mark of a great spirit to regard wrongs as beneath contempt: that the offender appear unworthy of having vengeance exacted from him is the most insulting sort of vengeance. Many people, while taking vengeance, have let trivial wrongs get more deeply under their skins: the great and notable man is the one who, like a great beast, listens without concern to small dogs' yapping.*
>
> SENECA,
On Anger

Clemency can avoid a present conflict and also set the initial conditions for a positive future relationship.

> *Think how a reputation for clemency will cause us to rise in others' estimation, and how many people pardon makes into useful friends.*
>
> SENECA,
On Anger

We should also consider a counter-factual where we do not exercise clemency. In this scenario, we allow anger to take control, and we decide to react by exacting harsh revenge. This might result in short-term satisfaction. But in the long term, this will come back to haunt us. From an ethical standpoint, we'll suffer from knowing that we didn't act virtuously. From a more practical standpoint, we'll always live in fear of retaliation.

> *To be feared is to fear: no one has been able to strike terror into others and at the same time enjoy peace of mind himself.*
>
> SENECA,
Moral Epistles, Letter 110

5. *De-escalate.* Certain situations intensify gradually before anger reaches a boiling point. Seneca advises to be alert to the initial stages of these escalations of anger. The goal is to stop these situations in the beginning, before they build up and our anger becomes harder to control.

> *Whenever a discussion turns overlong and quarrelsome, we should try to put a stop to it at the first stages before it gains strength. It's easier to abstain from a conflict than to extricate oneself.*
>
> SENECA,
On Anger

A conflict requires two sides. As the saying goes, "it takes two to tango." We should always remember this since it is in our control to avoid a confrontation.

> *Suppose someone becomes angry with you. You, by contrast, should challenge him to match you in kindness. Conflict subsides immediately when one party leaves it behind: there can be no fight without a pair of fighters.*
>
> Seneca,
On Anger

6. *Decatastrophize.* Lesson 17 presents another effective strategy to control our anger. People have the unfortunate habit of adding to their worries, making their situations worse than they have to be. A Stoic knows how to decatastrophize. The use of decatastrophizing techniques is a great way of keeping anger under control.

> *Many people manufacture their own causes for complaint through false suspicion and by exaggerating things that are trivial. Anger often comes to us, but we more often go to it.*
>
> Seneca,
On Anger

Seneca makes a forthright observation on this topic: some people act as if the intensity of their anger is an indication of its legitimacy.

> *We keep a grip on it and make it greater, as if being seriously angry proves that one is justly angry.*
>
> Seneca,
On Anger

If we don't decatastrophize, then the anger can far outlive its cause. We spend more time suffering from the consequences of anger than from what caused it.

We all spend more time being angry than being hurt.

SENECA,
On Anger

7. Delay. As Seneca himself said, there are two main goals regarding anger: to not fall into anger, and to not do wrong while angry. We've covered several mental techniques prescribed by him to keep us from falling into anger. But what if we fail? What if we are consumed by anger? How do we not do wrong while angry? First, we must accept that being angry doesn't have any upside. It has been suggested that anger, if properly channeled, can be used as motivation, or can become a booster for willpower. Seneca disagreed with this line of reasoning. According to him, anger cannot be controlled sufficiently to avoid its negative effects.

> *"Isn't it possible that we ought to take on anger as an ally because it has often been useful?" [...] Certain things are within our control at first, whereas the subsequent stages carry us along with a force all their own and leave us no way back. People who have jumped off a cliff cannot slow the descent of their bodies in freefall. [...] The best course is to reject the initial pricklings of anger, to fight against its first sparks, and to struggle not to succumb to it.*

SENECA,
On Anger

Musonius Rufus commented that a person consumed by anger cannot be reasoned with.

Words of advice and warning administered when a person's emotions are at their height and boiling over accomplish little or nothing.

MUSONIUS RUFUS,
From "The Moralia" by Plutarch

If anger cannot be used in an effective way, and if an angry person becomes impervious to reason, then what should we do if we are consumed by rage? Seneca had a simple suggestion:

> *The greatest remedy for anger is delay.*
>
> SENECA,
On Anger

When we are angry, we should refrain from doing anything. Seneca believed that the only wise response to anger is a self-imposed state of complete and utter inaction. We should stop whatever we are doing or planning on doing until the anger subsides. This was the same conclusion that the Greek philosopher Pythagoras had reached around five hundred years earlier.

> *In anger we should refrain both from speech and action.*
>
> PYTHAGORAS,
From "Lives and Opinions of Eminent Philosophers"
by Diogenes Laërtius, Book 8, Chapter 1

Anger is a dangerous emotion. Mental well-being requires an effective way of dealing with it. Stoicism teaches that nothing good comes out of being angry. Our goal is to control anger before it gains intensity. If we are overcome by it, we should refrain from action until it eases. A Turkish proverb wisely captures the destructive nature of anger: like sharp vinegar, anger damages its container.

Lesson 32

BE HUMBLE

Humility is a sign of wisdom, not weakness.

History is filled with examples of people remembered more by their humbleness (or lack thereof) than by their accomplishments. Lucius Quinctius Cincinnatus is one of them. A successful military leader of the early Roman Republic, Cincinnatus retired after decades of service and decided to spend his final years cultivating the land on his small farm. His plans were drastically altered in the year 458 BC. The Aequi, an Italic tribe that inhabited lands to the east, broke a peace treaty and invaded Roman lands. The two elected counsels (the highest positions in the Roman Republic) personally led armies against the rebellion, but both were surprisingly defeated. In panic, the Roman senators voted to elect a temporary dictator to lead the resistance against the invaders. Cincinnatus was named for a term of six months. It is said that upon receiving the news, Cincinnatus dressed himself with his old senatorial toga he had kept at a rustic cottage in the farm and made his way to the Senate to start his job. He defeated the Aequi in the Battle of Mount Algidus after only fifteen days and was greeted with a triumphal procession in his return to Rome. Some believed that Cincinnatus would want to stay in power. Instead, he immediately disbanded his army, resigned the dictatorship, and returned to his farm. The humbleness with which he accepted the call to assist Rome and then returned the power to the Senate is celebrated to this day.

Almost exactly one hundred years after Cincinnatus's virtuous actions, Herostratus showed how egotism can also guarantee eternal fame. He was a citizen of the Greek city of Ephesus, site of one of the Seven Wonders of the Ancient World: the Temple of Artemis. The poet Antipater of Sidon, one of the creators of the list of seven wonders, considered the temple to be the greatest of them all. Herostratus wanted his name to live and be immortalized forever. He decided to accomplish this by burning down the temple. At night, he set fire to the wooden roof beams, destroying it almost completely. Herostratus was captured and brought to justice. He was sentenced to the first *damnatio memoriae* (condemnation of memory) law in recorded history; the mere mention of his name in writing or speech was an offense punishable by death. Today, the term *Herostratic fame* means fame that is sought at any cost.

The contrasting examples of Cincinnatus and Herostratus illustrate the legacy-defining power of humility. Both men are still talked about 2,400 years after their deaths. Unfortunately, humility is deeply underestimated in modern Western societies. Psychological studies frequently rank it as one of the most appreciated personality traits, and yet there are influential cultural voices who claim that humility is a drawback in a modern world that rewards self-aggrandizement. It has even been labeled as a trait that stifles leadership. Stoicism thoroughly disagrees with this assessment. Stoic literature is awash with reminders to value humility.

1. Improvement. Marcus Aurelius's *Meditations* has over fifty passages with direct reminders to stay humble. Epictetus, despite being one of the most successful teachers of his time, advised against discussing philosophy in public, since it could be perceived as boasting. Stoic philosophy claims that humbleness is more than just a sociable personality trait. Humbleness is a key factor for personal improvement. Only those who recognize that they have room for improvement are open to bettering themselves. Epictetus claims that this should be the first attitude adopted by a philosopher.

The first thing a pretender to philosophy must do is get rid of their self-conceit; a person is not going to undertake to learn anything that they think they already know.

Epictetus,
Discourses, 2.17

True wisdom is only achieved with the assistance of correction mechanisms. Our goal should be to always improve ourselves. This entails the recognition of mistakes and a willingness to change. Seneca wrote about the foolishness of being attached to past positions.

It is not fickleness to abandon what you have recognized and condemned as an error; you have to declare honestly, "I thought something different; I was deceived." It belongs to the stubbornness of proud stupidity to say, "What I have once said, whatever it is, is to be an irrevocable law."

Seneca,
On Benefits, Book 4

Marcus Aurelius appreciated being corrected, which was highly unusual for the time. It was common for Roman Emperors to punish those who dared to say anything that went against their words. According to Marcus Aurelius, we are harmed by ignorance, not by truth.

If anyone can refute me—show me I'm making a mistake or looking at things from the wrong perspective—I'll gladly change. It's the truth I'm after, and the truth never harmed anyone. What harms us is to persist in self-deceit and ignorance.

Marcus Aurelius,
Meditations, 6.21

He makes an astute remark on this subject: it is inconsistent to try to escape the mistakes of others while being averse to fixing our own mistakes.

> *It is ridiculous not to escape from one's own vices, which is possible, while trying to escape the vices of others, which is impossible.*
>
> MARCUS AURELIUS,
Meditations, 7.71

2. *Assistance.* Asking for help isn't a sign of weakness. On the contrary, it is a sign of wisdom. We should have the humility to recognize when someone else can help us achieve an objective. This teaching is aligned with the Stoic concept of *sympatheia* and how we find happiness when we help each other. Marcus Aurelius compared it to soldiers on a mission.

> *Don't be ashamed to need help. Like a soldier storming a wall, you have a mission to accomplish. And if you've been wounded and need a comrade to pull you up? So what?*
>
> MARCUS AURELIUS,
Meditations, 7.7

Seneca considered the ability to take advice as crucial to living with virtue.

> *Virtue is to be willing and able to take advice.*
>
> SENECA,
On Benefits, Book 5

3. *Relationships.* Humility, or lack of it, is an influential factor in dictating the quality of our relationships. Arrogance is universally recognized as a negative personality trait. It wasn't by coincidence

that Dante Alighieri placed those who exhibit this trait at the ninth and central circle of hell. Seneca used an anecdote about Alexander the Great, who was notorious for his narcissism, to illustrate how arrogance can spoil even a good intention.

> *Alexander the Great, a madman whose plans were always on the epic scale, gave someone a city as a gift. The recipient took the measure of himself and tried to avoid the envy such a grand gift would attract by saying that it was not appropriate to his position. Alexander replied, "I do not consider what is fitting for you to accept, but only what is fitting for me to give."*
>
> SENECA,
> *On Benefits, Book 2*

Excess hubris can be dangerous. People who act with presumptuousness accumulate enemies over time. Not everyone is a Stoic; some of these enemies will not have the mental control to restrain themselves from trying to do harm. Seneca warned about how humbleness is a type of self-protection.

> *Even if by reason of tolerance we omit revenge, someone will arise to bring the impertinent, arrogant, and injurious man to punishment; for his offenses are never exhausted upon one individual or in one insult.*
>
> SENECA,
> *On the Firmness of the Wise Person*

But sometimes we need to give people a pass. When we are faced with someone lacking humility, we should remember that everyone commits mistakes. It takes humbleness to recognize that even our own actions might have come across as arrogant at some point. We should give others a generous allowance for error.

If we want to be fair judges in all matters, let's first convince ourselves that none of us is without fault. For this is the source of the greatest indignation, the thought "I'm without sin" and "I did nothing": no, rather, you admit nothing.

Seneca,
On Anger

Stoicism praises humbleness as a sign of wisdom and virtue. Many modern societies have forgotten about this teaching. It is the duty of a Stoic to show humility, even if the predominant culture of the time is too shortsighted to recognize how dignified it is.

Part 6

PRACTICE

―――⦾⦾⦾―――

*Just as wool takes up certain colors at once,
while there are others which it will not absorb unless it is
soaked and steeped in them many times; by men's minds
after once being accepted, but this system of which I speak,
unless it has gone deep and has sunk in for a long time,
and has not merely colored but thoroughly permeated
the soul, does not fulfill any of its promises.*

Seneca,
Moral Epistles, Letter 71

Lesson 33

PHILOSOPHY TAKES PRIORITY

Make time for philosophy.

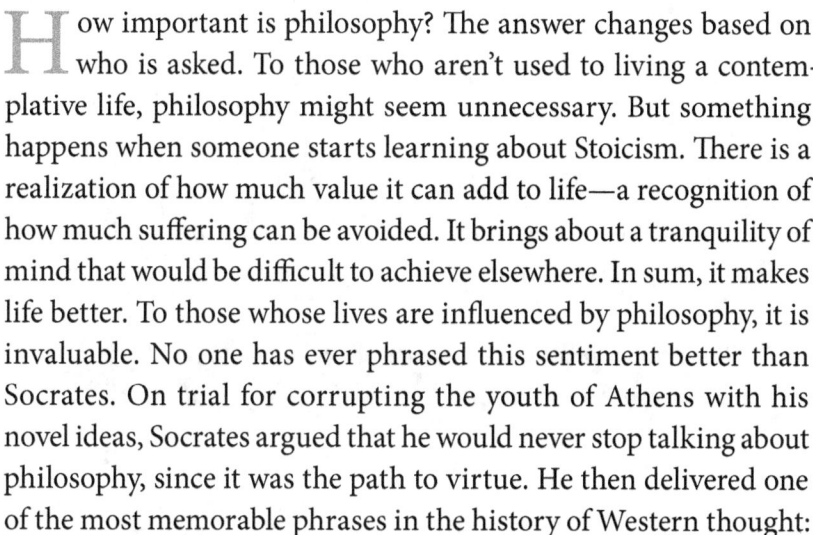

How important is philosophy? The answer changes based on who is asked. To those who aren't used to living a contemplative life, philosophy might seem unnecessary. But something happens when someone starts learning about Stoicism. There is a realization of how much value it can add to life—a recognition of how much suffering can be avoided. It brings about a tranquility of mind that would be difficult to achieve elsewhere. In sum, it makes life better. To those whose lives are influenced by philosophy, it is invaluable. No one has ever phrased this sentiment better than Socrates. On trial for corrupting the youth of Athens with his novel ideas, Socrates argued that he would never stop talking about philosophy, since it was the path to virtue. He then delivered one of the most memorable phrases in the history of Western thought:

> *The unexamined life is not worth living.*
>
> Socrates,
> *Apology of Socrates*, by Plato

1. Priority. Philosophy is life-altering to its practitioners. To Socrates, life without it was unacceptable. We should value and prioritize it in accordance with the benefits we get out of it. Philosophy shouldn't be something that we do in our spare time, whenever we have a break from our other daily tasks. We need to make time for philosophy. It should be the main priority; everything else should be planned around it. In one of my personal favorite Stoic quotes, Seneca used an anecdote from Alexander the Great to make this point.

> *When some state or other offered Alexander a part of its territory and half of its property he told them that 'he hadn't come to Asia with the intention of accepting whatever they cared to give him, but of letting them keep whatever he chose to leave them.' Philosophy, likewise, tells all other occupations: 'It's not my intention to accept whatever time is left over from you; you shall have, instead, what I reject.'*
>
> SENECA,
Moral Epistles, Letter 53

Living a life that prioritizes philosophy will have its challenges. It will require constant reading. It will demand studying and putting what we learn into practice. But given the size of the reward, isn't it worth it?

> *Will we not summon our endurance when such a great prize awaits us, the undisturbed tranquility of a joyful mind?*
>
> SENECA,
On Anger

2. *Guidance*. Life can be confusing. We never know what the future holds. Things are one way today and completely different tomorrow. To makes things more complicated, there is no easy guide to living a good life. Seneca wrote about how the journey of life is singularly challenging.

> *The conditions of this journey are different from those of most*

travel. On most journeys some well-recognized road and inquiries made of the inhabitants of the region prevent you from going astray; but on this one all the best beaten and the most frequented paths are the most deceptive.

SENECA,
On the Happy Life

Stoicism gives us invaluable advice on how to navigate this complex landscape. Without it, we can feel lost, at the mercy of the tides of fate and at the whims of our evolutionary impulses.

If a man knows not to which port he sails, no wind is favorable.

SENECA,
Moral Epistles, Letter 71

When a person is following a track, there is an eventual end somewhere, but with wandering at large there is no limit.

SENECA,
Moral Epistles, Letter 16

3. **Wisdom.** Fame, success, fortune, status. These are the things that most people seek. But those who achieve them quickly realize that these things don't necessarily lead to a good life. True happiness can only be achieved through wisdom. A life of philosophy is the path to *eudaimonia*. Marcus Aurelius pointed to the difference in quality of life between philosophers and great conquerors from antiquity.

Alexander and Caesar and Pompey. Compared to Diogenes, Heraclitus, Socrates? The philosophers knew the what, the why, the how. Their minds were their own. The others? Nothing but anxiety and enslavement.

MARCUS AURELIUS,
Meditations, 8.3

The wisdom from Stoicism has endured the test of time. We are fortunate to have the thoughts of great minds from the past to help us improve our lives today.

> *Honors, statues and all other mighty monuments to man's ambition carved in stone will crumble but the wisdom of the past is indestructible. Age cannot wither nor destroy the knowledge which serves all generations.*
>
> Seneca,
> *On the Shortness of Life*

The only way of benefiting from all that philosophy has to offer is by continuously giving it preference over other things that compete for our attention. Everyone wants to live a happy life. We all wish to achieve *eudaimonia*. And yet oftentimes we prioritize trivial tasks over the one thing that can give us what we want the most. Stoicism should come first.

Lesson 34

LEARN FOR YOURSELF

Self-improvement benefits all.

German philosopher Gottfried Wilhelm Leibniz once wrote an essay in which he mentioned a "sect of the new Stoics" whose ideas had become influential during the Age of Enlightenment. Leibniz claimed that the head of this sect was a philosopher considered today as one of the most important of the last five hundred years: Baruch Spinoza. Born in Amsterdam in 1632, Spinoza came from a family of Portuguese Jewish descent who had escaped religious persecution in Portugal by moving to the Netherlands (at the time known as the Dutch Republic). He was a rationalist freethinker who was excommunicated from the Jewish community of Amsterdam because of his biblical criticism, considered an "abominable heresy." His secular philosophical views were incompatible with the orthodoxy of the religion that surrounded him.

Spinoza spent most of his life as a solitary academic. He refused an offer to teach philosophy at Heidelberg University, replying that "I do not know how to teach philosophy without becoming a disturber of the peace." He earned a modest living from making optical lenses, including the telescopic lenses used by astronomer Christiaan Huygens when he proved that Saturn is encircled by rings and discovered the moon Titan. Spinoza didn't claim to be a Stoic, but his philosophy was heavily influenced by Stoicism. He based his ethics on the belief that emotions depend on human judgments. He even had his own version of *premeditatio malorum*. More notably, Spinoza embodied the ideals of a core Stoic notion: wisdom has intrinsic value, and therefore the act of learning is virtuous in and of itself. Stoicism claims that the acquisition of knowledge is valuable on a standalone basis. Spinoza understood this. The persecution against his philosophy didn't stop him from continuing to learn, even if it meant that he had to learn for himself. He expressed this idea in one of the few essays he published in life.

> *After experience had taught me that all the usual surroundings of social life are vain and futile, [...] I finally resolved to inquire [...] whether, in fact, there might be anything of which the discovery and attainment would enable me to enjoy continuous, supreme, and unending happiness.*
>
> BARUCH SPINOZA,
On the Improvement of the Understanding

Spinoza's *magnum opus*, the philosophical treatise *Ethics*, was published posthumously. He wasn't looking for fame. He didn't seek wealth. The man who influenced virtually all Western philosophers who came after him was content with improving himself.

1. *Self-improvement.* Learning leads to wisdom, and wisdom is the path to mental well-being. The act of learning is an active step toward a better life. Some people carry the misconception that knowledge should be flaunted. Or at the very least, it should translate into some practical action that can be observed by others. Stoicism teaches that the true value of wisdom comes from self-improvement.

> *For whose benefit, then, did I learn it all? If it was for your own benefit that you learnt it you have no call to fear that your trouble may have been wasted.*
>
> SENECA,
Moral Epistles, Letter 7

The idea of accomplishing something for the pure sake of self-improvement isn't limited to just academic learning. Performing a task well, to the best of one's ability, is also a manner of self-improvement. Seneca tells an anecdote of an artist whose work wasn't exhibited to large audiences. The wise artist didn't care; what mattered to him was the mental well-being he extracted from the act of working on his craft.

> *Good is the answer given by the person, whoever it was (his identity was uncertain), who when asked what was the object of all the trouble he took over a piece of craftmanship when it would never reach more than a very few people, replied: "A few is enough for me; so is one; so is none."*
>
> SENECA,
Moral Epistles, Letter 7

Seneca expanded on this idea by using an example with Phidias, the legendary Greek artist credited with sculpting the Statue of Zeus at Olympia, one of the Seven Wonders of the Ancient World. Seneca draws a distinction between what Phidias gets out of producing art and what he gets from the artistic piece itself. From the act of producing art, Phidias achieves a positive mental state. This is sufficient reward for the wise. From the piece of art itself, Phidias might extract an additional bonus such as recognition, fame, or money.

> *Phidias makes a statue. The reward from his art is one thing; the reward from his work of art is something else. Having done what he aimed to do is the reward from his art; having done so with profits is the reward from his work of art. Even if Phidias has not sold his work, he has completed it. So there are three kinds of reward from his work: one comes from his awareness, and this he got when he finished the work; another comes from reputation; and the third comes in the form of some practical payoff, which will come either from good will,*

from the sale of the work, or from some other advantage.

Seneca,
On Benefits, Book 2

2. Interconnectedness. The concept of seeking wisdom for self-improvement might sound selfish. Some might argue that it is inconsistent with other Stoic teachings that encourage us to improve others. Seneca addressed this issue in his essay *On Leisure*. According to Seneca, we should remember what the concepts of cosmopolitanism and *sympatheia* entail: we are all interconnected and mutually dependent. Therefore, the person who seeks self-improvement also benefits those around him, since he becomes a more valuable asset for society as a whole.

> *Just as the man that chooses to become worse injures not only himself but all those whom, if he had become better, he might have benefited, so whoever wins the approval of himself benefits others by the very fact that he prepares what will prove beneficial to them.*

Seneca,
On Leisure

It is certainly desirable for someone to use his wisdom to benefit others, but many don't have an opportunity to do so. This doesn't mean that they aren't participating in the betterment of their communities. Self-improvement is a form of social responsibility.

> *It is of course required of a man that he should benefit his fellow-men—many if he can; if not, a few; if not a few, those who are nearest; if not these, himself. For when he renders himself useful to others, he engages in public affairs.*

Seneca,
On Leisure

Epictetus agreed with this point. It isn't necessary to be a wealthy, philanthropic benefactor to make a difference. Someone who focuses on becoming wiser also benefits his community.

> *"But my community will be helpless—to the extent that I can help." Again, what kind of help do you have in mind? You can't give building or baths, but so what? The blacksmith can't give it shoes, nor can the cobbler supply it with arms. It's enough if everyone plays their respective part. I mean, wouldn't you benefit your community by adding another lawful and loyal citizen to its rolls? "Yes." Then evidently you have it in you to benefit it all on your own.*
>
> Epictetus,
Enchiridion, Chapter 24

The purpose of wisdom isn't to impress. It isn't necessary to broadcast the steps we take for self-improvement. Be content with learning for yourself. It will improve your life—and the lives of everyone around you.

Lesson 35

Excellence Is a Habit

*Wisdom is learned through
continuous improvement.*

It is virtually impossible to write a book that involves Greek philosophy without mentioning Aristotle. Few people have had as profound an influence over Western thought. His teachings spanned across multiple subjects, from philosophy to physics to theater. His significance to Christian theology was so strong that Thomas Aquinas referred to him as "The Philosopher." Zeno of Citium founded the Stoic school about twenty years after the death of Aristotle. There were several practical and theoretical differences between Stoicism and the teachings of the Peripatetic school, the name given to the school of philosophy founded by Aristotle. But they also shared some striking similarities, starting with the origin of their names: Stoicism is named after the Stoa Poikile, the colonnaded building where Zeno taught his followers. Peripatetic comes from *peripatoi*, the walkways inside the Lyceum temple were Aristotle liked to teach. Both schools share some foundational philosophical assumptions. As an example, both claim that wisdom should be a path toward *eudaimonia*. One area where the similarities are particularly striking is in their views of the process of achieving wisdom. Some contemporary philosophies claimed that wisdom was an innate characteristic—some are born to be wise, while others aren't. The Stoics and the Peripatetics believed in continuous improvement. The *Nicomachean Ethics*, Aristotle's best-known work on ethics, emphasizes the importance of repetition in the path toward wisdom.

> *Activity must occupy a complete lifetime; for one swallow does not make spring, nor does one fine day; and similarly one day or a brief period of happiness does not make a man supremely blessed and happy.*
>
> Aristotle,
> *Nicomachean Ethics*, Book 1, Section 7

> *Virtues we get by first exercising them, as happens in the case of the arts as well. For the things we have to learn before we can do them, we learn by doing them. Men become builders by building and lyre players by playing the lyre; so too we become just by doing just acts, temperate by doing temperate acts, brave by doing brave acts.*
>
> Aristotle,
> *Nicomachean Ethics*, Book 2, Section 1

Pulitzer Prize-winning philosopher and historian Will Durant elegantly paraphrased the essence of Aristotle's thoughts:

> *We are what we repeatedly do. Excellence, then, is not an act but a habit.*
>
> Will Durant [paraphrasing Aristotle],
> *The Story of Philosophy*, Chapter 2, Section 7

1. Repetition. Stoicism is in complete alignment with Aristotle on the significance of repetition. Stoic literature is filled with passages on how learning philosophy is a lengthy process. It takes time, effort, discipline, and multiple iterations to learn. We cannot expect to become Stoic masters in a short period of time. Musonius Rufus

talked about this. Some of his teachings are indistinguishable from excerpts from Aristotle's *Nicomachean Ethics*.

> *A person who has not studied letters, music, or sports does not say that he knows them. Nor does he pretend to possess these skills if he is unable to name also the teacher to whom he went. So why do we all declare that we have virtue? A human being has no claim by nature to any of those other skills, and no one comes into life with a natural ability for them.*
>
> Musonius Rufus,
Lectures included in the Anthology
by Joannes Stobaeus

Musonius pointed to philosophy as an area of study that requires even more continuous practice than others.

> *The person who claims to be studying philosophy must practice it even more diligently than the person who aspires to the art of medicine or some similar skill, inasmuch as philosophy is more important and harder to grasp than any other pursuit. People who study skills other than philosophy have not been previously corrupted in their souls by learning things contrary to what they are about to learn, but people who attempt to study philosophy, since they have been already in the midst of much corruption and are filled with evil, pursue virtue in such a condition that they need even more practice in it.*
>
> Musonius Rufus,
Lectures included in the Anthology
by Joannes Stobaeus

Seneca also wrote on this topic. He encouraged new Stoics to continue studying with devotion until the lessons fully sunk in and became second nature.

[On the practice of philosophy] Keep a hold on it and put it on a firm footing, so that what is at present an enthusiasm may become a settled spiritual disposition.

Seneca,
Moral Epistles, Letter 16

2. Don't give up. The process of learning Stoicism isn't a smooth upward-trending line. It is filled with peaks and valleys, successes and failures. Many people feel demotivated when they realize how difficult it is to follow the Stoic teachings that they read and appreciate. But that's the way it is for everyone. Philosophy is hard. We, mere mortals, aren't the only ones who struggle. Marcus Aurelius himself included several self-reminders in his *Meditations* urging himself to not give up.

Not to feel exasperated, or defeated, or despondent because your days aren't packed with wise and moral actions. But to get back up when you fail, to celebrate behaving like a human—however imperfectly—and fully embrace the pursuit you've embarked on.

Marcus Aurelius,
Meditations, 5.9

He suggested that we should recognize our shortcomings and then be done with them. Every day is a new day and a new opportunity to try again. We shouldn't let our past deviations from philosophy haunt us in the present.

You can't claim to have lived your life as a philosopher—not even your whole adulthood. You can see for yourself how far you are from philosophy. And so can many others. […] Now forget what they think of you. Be satisfied if you can live the rest of your life, however short, as your nature demands.

Focus on that, and don't let anything distract you.

MARCUS AURELIUS,
Meditations, 8.1

The most encouraging words on this topic come from Seneca. He observed that Stoicism doesn't come equally to everyone. Some people have personalities that are more naturally inclined to acting stoically. He believed that these people were the most fortunate but not the ones who deserved the most praise. The ones who deserve full admiration are the ones who must battle their own innate predispositions on the path to achieve wisdom.

> *I would say, therefore, that although the person who has no difficulty with himself is indeed more fortunate, the more deserving on his own account is the one who has overcome the shortcomings of his own nature, not just making his way toward wisdom but actually dragging himself there.*

SENECA,
Moral Epistles, Letter 52

3. *Perfection.* What is the final stage in this process of continuous improvement? When do we reach Stoic perfection? The answer is short and blunt: never. The Stoic Wise Man, who always acts with virtue and lives a life of complete *eudaimonia*, is just an idealized archetype. Even the most prominent Stoic philosophers recognize that they are far from perfect. Seneca compared himself to someone lying in a hospital bed while giving advice to other sick patients.

> *I'm not so shameless as to undertake to heal others while sick myself. It is rather as if we were lying in the same hospital room; I'm talking with you about our common illness, and sharing remedies. So listen to me as though I were talking to*

myself. I'm letting you into my private place, and am examining myself, using you as a foil.

Seneca,
Moral Epistles, Letter 27

A Stoic shouldn't benchmark himself against a theoretical godlike wise man; the true comparison should be against our past selves.

I am not a wise man, nor shall I ever be. And so require not from me that I should be equal to the best, but that I should be better than the wicked. It is enough for me if every day I reduce the number of my vices, and blame my mistakes.

Seneca,
On the Happy Life

Epictetus acknowledged that he would never be as great a philosopher as Socrates. That wasn't a reason to stop his process of self-improvement. It is unreasonable to stop a pursuit just because of fear of not being the greatest of all at it.

I will not be better than Socrates. I will never be Milo either; nevertheless, I don't neglect my body. Nor will I be another Croesus—and still, I don't neglect my property. In short, we do not abandon any discipline for despair of not being the best in it.

Epictetus,
Discourses, 1.2

Old age isn't a reason to stop either. Our pursuit for wisdom should continue all the way to our last moments. There is a famous anecdote on this topic about Diogenes the Cynic. One of the founders of the Cynic school of philosophy, Diogenes passed on his teachings to his student Crates of Thebes, who in turn was Zeno of Citium's teacher before he founded the Stoic school.

> *To those who said to Diogenes the Cynic, "You are an old man; take a rest," he replied, "if I were running in the stadium, ought I to slacken my pace when approaching the goal? Ought I not rather to put on speed?"*
>
> DIOGENES THE CYNIC,
> *From "Lives and Opinions of Eminent Philosophers" by Diogenes Laërtius, Book 6, Chapter 2*

4. *Celebrate.* We've established that learning philosophy is hard, takes time, will lead to failures, and on top of all that the process will never be fully perfected. This doesn't sound like much fun. Turns out that this process is extremely fulfilling. Even Epictetus, who certainly wasn't known for having a bubbly personality, said that this journey gives us reasons to celebrate every day.

> *Be happy when you find that doctrines you have learned and analyzed are being tested by real events. If you've succeeded in removing or reducing the tendency to be mean and critical, or thoughtless, or foul-mouthed, or careless, or nonchalant; if old interests no longer engage you, at least not to the same extent; then every day can be a feast day—today because you acquitted yourself well in one set of circumstances, tomorrow because of another. How much better cause is this to celebrate than becoming consul or governor; because you have yourself to thank.*
>
> EPICTETUS,
> *Discourses, 4.4*

Philosophy isn't learned overnight. The road to wisdom is long and winding but filled with rewards along the way. We might never reach perfection, but we can strive to get as close to it as possible. Wisdom isn't something you're born with—it is something you learn. Seneca summarized it well:

No man was ever wise by chance.

SENECA,
Moral Epistles, Letter 76

Lesson 36

ACTIONS, NOT WORDS

Philosophy needs to be acted out.

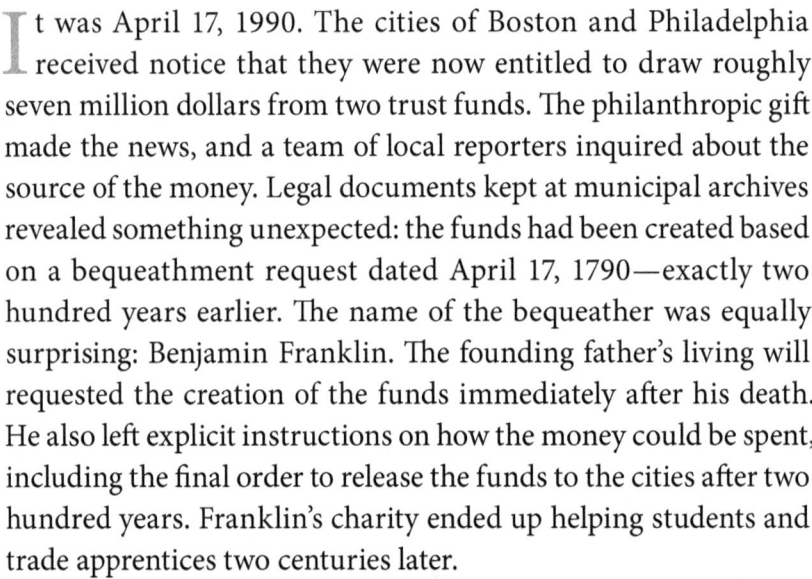

It was April 17, 1990. The cities of Boston and Philadelphia received notice that they were now entitled to draw roughly seven million dollars from two trust funds. The philanthropic gift made the news, and a team of local reporters inquired about the source of the money. Legal documents kept at municipal archives revealed something unexpected: the funds had been created based on a bequeathment request dated April 17, 1790—exactly two hundred years earlier. The name of the bequeather was equally surprising: Benjamin Franklin. The founding father's living will requested the creation of the funds immediately after his death. He also left explicit instructions on how the money could be spent, including the final order to release the funds to the cities after two hundred years. Franklin's charity ended up helping students and trade apprentices two centuries later.

This curious event was an example of the desire to act that characterized Ben Franklin throughout his life. He was considered the most accomplished American of his time because of his relentless drive to make a difference. He was, among other things, an inventor, scientist, author, politician, diplomat, philanthropist, and postmaster. Between 1732 and 1758, he published a popular yearly almanac named *Poor Richard's Almanac*. The almanac was a glimpse into his inexhaustible nature and included a plethora of subjects that Franklin believed would be useful and entertaining to his readers. His witticisms were a favorite of the public. Although Franklin never self-described as a Stoic, many of his actions and words embodied Stoic values. The 1737 edition of his almanac included a particularly Stoic aphorism:

Well done is better than well said.

BENJAMIN FRANKLIN,
Poor Richard's Almanac, 1737 Edition

1. *Action*. Stoic texts have captivated readers for millennia. However, the Stoic philosophers didn't write to impress. They wrote to drive action. Stoic philosophy isn't meant to be a mindless read—it must be acted out. Musonius Rufus was known for requiring his students to exemplify what they learned.

Only by exhibiting actions in harmony with the sound words which he has received will anyone be helped by philosophy.

MUSONIUS RUFUS,
*Lectures included in the Anthology
by Joannes Stobaeus*

Musonius Rufus's most famous student was Epictetus, who unquestionably learned the lesson taught by his mentor. Once he became a teacher himself, Epictetus's teachings were filled with reminders that memorizing Stoic quotes was worthless if it didn't lead to the embodiment of Stoic action. He compared it to an athlete who was proud of his dumbbells instead of his body.

So who is making progress—the person who has read many of Chrysippus' books? Is virtue no more than this—to become literate in Chrysippus? [...] If you aim to be perfect when you are still anxious and apprehensive, how have you made

> *progress? So let's see some evidence of it. But no, it's as if I were to say to an athlete, "Show me your shoulders," and he responded with, "Have a look at my weights." "Get out of here with your gigantic weights!" I'd say, "What I want to see isn't the weights but how you've profited from using them."*
>
> Epictetus,
Discourses, 1.4

Epictetus was a harsh critic of those who use philosophy to try to impress. He frequently accused his students of going around town repeating what they learned in his class just to boast. He reminded them that using philosophy for this purpose was missing the point.

> *Even now, if the opportunity presents itself, I know you will go off to read and make public those compositions, and you'll pride yourself on being fluent in dialogue form. Don't do it. What I would rather hear from you is, "Look how I don't fail in my desires, or have experiences I don't want. I'll prove it to you in the case of death, I'll prove it to you in the case of physical pain, in the case of prison, of condemnation, of ill repute." That's the real test of a youth fit to finish school. Forget about that other stuff, don't let people hear you giving public recitations; and even if someone praises you, restrain yourself, be content to look like a nobody or a know-nothing.*
>
> Epictetus,
Discourses, 2.1

2. *Courage*. Fear is one of the main impediments to action. Many people refrain from doing what is right because of fear of backlash. This posture is sometimes described as a way of staying "free" from undesirable circumstances. Seneca reminds us that inaction based on fear is not liberty.

> *From the fear of insults or from weariness of them, we shall fall short in the doing of many needful things, and, suffering from a distaste for hearing anything not to our mind, we shall refuse to face both public and private duties, sometimes even when they are for our well-being. [...] But not to put up with anything is not liberty; we deceive ourselves.*
>
> SENECA,
> *On the Firmness of the Wise Person*

It requires courage to act according to Stoicism. We will sometimes face harsh criticism. Some will try to smear our intentions. We cannot forget that all honorable action is faced with this type of reaction. Stoicism teaches that we shouldn't be affected by the response we get from others. As Seneca says, these attacks shouldn't pierce through our helmet.

> *The more honorable a man is, the more heroically he should bear himself, remembering that the tallest ranks stand in the front battleline. Let him bear insults, shameful words, civil disgrace, and all other degradation as he would the enemy's war cry, and the darts and stones from afar that rattle around a soldier's helmet but cause no wound.*
>
> SENECA,
> *On the Firmness of the Wise Person*

We should view potential criticism to our actions from the perspective of the Trichotomy of Control. Criticism is an external—something we do not control. When we act, our goal is to try to do our best. That's the part that we control. Nothing else matters.

Remember that our efforts are subject to circumstances; you weren't aiming to do the impossible. "Aiming to do what, then?" To try. And you succeeded. What you set out to do is accomplished.

MARCUS AURELIUS,
Meditations, 6.50

Fear isn't a valid excuse for inaction. Reciting quotes isn't a valid reason to learn philosophy. We need to embody what we learn, act out what Stoic philosophy tells us to do. Less talking. More doing. Marcus Aurelius demanded it from himself:

Waste no more time arguing what a good man should be. Be one.

MARCUS AURELIUS,
Meditations, 10.16

Lesson 37

Protect Your Time

*Make time for yourself by using
your time wisely.*

Most months of the year are named after Roman gods. March is named after Mars, god of war. May after Maia, goddess of growth. June comes from the goddess of marriage and childbirth, Juno. Only two months are named after real people. July was named to celebrate Julius Caesar. August was an honor bestowed upon the man considered one of the most successful leaders to ever live: Julius Caesar's great-nephew and adoptive son, Caesar Augustus. He was the first emperor of the Roman Empire; a position he earned after winning the civil war that broke out following the assassination of Julius Caesar. The empire doubled in size during Augustus's reign, and its new structure ensured a rare period of peace that would go on to last two hundred years.

It was in recognition of such accomplishments that the Roman Senate issued an extraordinary *senatus consultum* (senate decree) in the year 8 BC, declaring that the month in which Augustus had achieved his major feats would be renamed August. It was also decided that August couldn't be shorter than any other month, and therefore from that point onward it would increase from thirty to thirty-one days. The extra day would be removed from February, which was already the shortest month with twenty-nine days, and would now have only twenty-eight.

Augustus ruled with absolute unchecked control over the empire. The fact that the calendar changed in his honor shows the extent of his power. And yet, he didn't have the thing he desired the most: time for himself. Augustus yearned for the day in which his duties as emperor wouldn't keep him from doing the things he genuinely appreciated in life. He was aware that this day would likely never arrive. As consequence, he developed the peculiar habit of talking constantly about this future day he wished for. It was almost as if it served as motivation to work in the present so that maybe it could become a reality at some point. In his essay *On the Shortness of Life*, Seneca quoted a passage from a letter Augustus wrote to the Roman Senate on this topic:

> *My deep desire for that time, which I have long prayed for, has led me to anticipate something of its delight by the pleasure of words, since the joy of that reality is still slow in coming.*
>
> SENECA [QUOTING AUGUSTUS],
> *On the Shortness of Life*

1. Waste. Seneca described Augustus's desire for spare time as a "recurring day-dream in which he [Augustus] found escape from his burdens." Seneca's writing indicates that he felt some empathy toward Augustus, but he certainly didn't see much wisdom in his mindset. Stoicism teaches that the problem isn't that we don't have enough time; the problem is that we don't use our time wisely.

> *The problem is not that we have a short life, but that we waste time. [...] The time we are given is not brief, but we make it so. We do not lack time; on the contrary, there is so much of it that we waste an obscene amount.*
>
> SENECA,
> *On the Shortness of Life*

We spend our lives devoting too much time to unnecessary things. According to Seneca, most of our existence is just time; little of it is actually lived.

> *The amount of life we truly live is small. For our existence on Earth is not Life, but merely Time.*
>
> Seneca,
On the Shortness of Life

Some reach old age without having lived much.

> *A grey-haired wrinkled man has not necessarily lived long. More accurately, he has existed long.*
>
> Seneca,
On the Shortness of Life

2. *Personal time.* One of our main mistakes is that we don't leave enough time for ourselves. We fill up our schedules with many different types of tasks and forget to schedule personal time.

> *Count, I say, and review the days of your life; you will see that very few have been devoted to yourself.*
>
> Seneca,
On the Shortness of Life

Seneca makes an interesting observation about a common double standard we're guilty of committing. We often complain when someone doesn't devote enough time to us; a boss, a friend, a family member—they don't give us the attention we deserve. But we don't give ourselves the personal time we need either.

> *How can anyone complain that no one will devote time to them when they allot no time for themselves?*
>
> Seneca,
On the Shortness of Life

3. **Interruptions.** Why are people so bad at protecting their own time? A primary factor is that we do a terrible job of protecting our time from others. We get side-tracked by other people's words, engrossed by their thoughts, angry at their actions. We don't allow others to steal our possessions, but we allow them to take away our time, a much more precious asset.

> *People don't let others steal their property, and they rush to vigorously defend themselves if there is even the slightest controversy over the demarcation of land boundaries, yet they allow others to trespass on their very existence.*
>
> Seneca,
On the Shortness of Life

We're also notoriously bad at saying "no." We are frequently interrupted. We attend events we don't want to attend. All these intrusions into our time accumulate, and we're left with little time for ourselves. Stoicism advises us to get into the habit of saying "no" more often. The more we say "no" to others, the more we can say "yes" to ourselves.

> *In protecting their wealth men are tight-fisted, but when it comes to the matter of time, in the case of the one thing in which it is wise to be parsimonious, they are actually generous to a fault.*
>
> Seneca,
On the Shortness of Life

4. *Procrastination.* We're guilty of procrastinating. Seneca reminds us that we shouldn't take time for granted. Nothing guarantees that we will be around for much longer. We live as if we are immortals but then reach the end of our lives complaining that we didn't have enough time to do what we wished.

> *You live as if you will live forever, no care for your mortality ever enters your head, you pay no mind to how much time has already gone by. You waste time as if it was a limitless resource, when any moment you spend on someone else or some matter is potentially your last.*
>
> SENECA,
On the Shortness of Life

We would procrastinate less if we could see how much time is left ahead of us.

> *If each man could see the number of years he has left ahead, just as he can see the years he has behind him, how disturbed those would be who saw only a few left, how careful they would be with them!*
>
> SENECA,
On the Shortness of Life

5. *Prioritize.* The most efficient way of freeing up time is to develop the habit of prioritizing things appropriately. Marcus Aurelius wrote extensively on this subject. As emperor of Rome, he knew that there was never any shortage of things to do, so he started doing what Augustus should have done roughly two hundred years before him: he started eliminating unnecessary tasks from his schedule and focusing exclusively on the most important items.

> *Most of what we say and do is not essential. If you can eliminate it, you'll have more time, and more tranquility. Ask yourself at every moment, "Is this necessary?"*
>
> MARCUS AURELIUS,
Meditations, 4.24

He noticed that the attention devoted to something should be proportional to its importance. This is another area where most people use their time unwisely: we waste too much time focusing on topics that have almost no real bearing over our lives.

> *The value of attentiveness varies in proportion to its object. You're better off not giving the small things more time than they deserve.*
>
> MARCUS AURELIUS,
Meditations, 4.32

Seneca considered curiosity to be potentially damaging in this regard. Many people go to great lengths in search of everything that is said about them. Or they go after gossip and overall meddling into other people's lives. They cast out a very wide net in search of information and then are consumed by what they find when they pull it back in. This is an unnecessary exercise. We should focus more on what truly matters and less on frivolities.

> *It's not a good idea to hear and see everything that goes on. Let many injuries just pass us by: the person who doesn't register most of them doesn't suffer them. You don't want to be inclined to anger? Don't be inquisitive.*
>
> SENECA,
On Anger

Marcus Aurelius eloquently defined his goal in a short maxim:

To do less, better.

MARCUS AURELIUS,
Meditations, 4.24

Time is a precious asset. We have more than enough of it as long as we use it wisely. Time spent angry at those we disapprove of could be better employed in the company of those we admire. The time we waste in procrastination would be better spent practicing philosophy. Stoicism teaches that we should protect our time—from others and also from our own wastefulness.

Lesson 38

WATCH THE WISE

Role models add to our wisdom.

Albert Einstein lived in a cottage-style house in Princeton, New Jersey, from 1936 until his death in 1955. He appreciated the simplicity of the house: just a plain two-story construction that blended seamlessly with all the others in the street. Einstein spent most of his time in a small study room filled from floor to ceiling with books. The wall next to his desk was decorated with portraits of three men: Isaac Newton, Michael Faraday, and James Clerk Maxwell. They were Einstein's role models. At many points throughout his life, Einstein voiced how important these three scientists were to him. He wrote an essay in which he described his appreciation for them on the centenary of Maxwell's birth in 1931.

> *The greatest change in the axiomatic basis of physics, and correspondingly in our conception of the structure of reality, since the foundation of theoretical physics through Newton, came about through the researches of Faraday and Maxwell on electromagnetic phenomena.*
>
> ALBERT EINSTEIN,
*Maxwell's Influence on the Development
of the Conception of Physical Reality*, 1931

Einstein had written a similar letter four years earlier at the bicentennial of Newton's death. The letter was sent to the King's School in Lincolnshire, England, where Newton was educated. Einstein wasn't shy with praise for Newton.

> *He was not only an inventor of genius in respect of particular guiding methods; he also showed a unique mastery of the empirical material known in his time, and he was marvelously inventive in special mathematical and physical demonstrations. For all these reasons he deserves our deep veneration.*
>
> ALBERT EINSTEIN,
> On Newton, 1927

Isaac Newton was also highly appreciative of his role models. In a letter written to fellow physicist Robert Hooke, Newton expressed how his novel theories were only possible due to the contributions of the great minds he admired.

> *If I have seen farther, it is by standing on the shoulders of giants.*
>
> ISAAC NEWTON,
> Letter to Robert Hooke, 1675

Two of these giants were Johannes Kepler and Galileo Galilei. Newton explicitly writes about his reverence for them in his *magnum opus*, the 1687 book *Philosophiae Naturalis Principia Mathematica*. One hundred years earlier, Kepler and Galileo exchanged correspondence where they agreed on the person who they looked up to: Nicolaus Copernicus.

1. *Role models.* The cycle of thinkers who were made better by what they learned from their role models extends all the way back to the beginnings of humanity. The ability to learn from mentors

is one of the defining differences between humans and all other animals. This intergenerational exchange of knowledge is at the basis of civilization. Stoic philosophy puts great emphasis on the value of learning from role models.

> *Choose someone whose way of life as well as words, and whose very face as mirroring the character that lies behind it, have won your approval. Be always pointing him out to yourself either as your guardian or as your model. There is a need, in my view, for someone as a standard against which our characters can measure themselves. Without a ruler to do it against you won't make crooked straight.*
>
> SENECA,
Moral Epistles, Letter 11

Some of our role models might be historical figures or the great minds in our fields of study. Others might be family members, mentors, or acquaintances who have a strong impact over our lives. Copernicus was deeply inspired by his uncle, Lucas Watzenrode, who was a fatherly figure and always supported his studies. Our biological parents are set by nature, but we can choose the role models that we aspire to emulate.

> *They say 'you can't choose your parents,' that they have been given to us by chance; but the good news is we can choose to be the sons of whomever we desire. There are many respectable fathers scattered across the centuries to choose from. Select a genius and make yourself their intellectual heir.*
>
> SENECA,
On the Shortness of Life

2. *Wisdom.* Role models add to our wisdom. They are like scouts who explore a path before us and then come back to report what

they've learned. We can benefit from their knowledge without being exposed to the challenges inherent in gathering such knowledge.

> *What bliss, what a glorious old age awaits the man who has offered himself as a mate to these intellects! He will have mentors and colleagues from whom he may seek advice on the smallest of matters, companions ever ready with counsel for his daily life, from whom he may hear truth without judgment, praise without flattery, and after whose likeness he may fashion himself.*
>
> SENECA,
On the Shortness of Life

They allow us to be wise beyond our years. We can aggregate their wisdom to ours. With their help, we can gather the knowledge that would've taken hundreds, or even thousands of years for a single person to accumulate.

> *It is fair to say that those who make Zeno, Pythagoras, Democritus and other giants of philosophy their daily companions will be more fully engaged in a rewarding life. [...] None of these men will bring about your death any time sooner, but rather they will teach you how to die. None of them will shorten your lifespan, but each will add the wisdom of his years to yours.*
>
> SENECA,
On the Shortness of Life

3. Actions. How should we pick a role model? How can we know that we aren't misguided, and that the person we look up to is truly worth emulating? It goes without saying that we should follow the example of people who we believe acted with wisdom. But a key lesson is that we should value more highly those who acted, and not only spoke.

> *Choose as your helper someone you admire more when you see him than when you listen to him.*
>
> SENECA,
> *Moral Epistles, Letter 52*

We should appreciate those who act with virtue. The emphasis should be on the quality of the actions, not on whether such actions accomplished their desired goals. History is full of examples of virtuous people worth emulating who didn't succeed in a stated objective. Stoicism teaches that the only goals worth having are the ones that depend exclusively on what we control. Someone might fail to climb a mountain or to cross a desert, but he might still accomplish the goal of trying his best or of attacking the objective with determination. To a Stoic, that is what matters.

> *Look up to those who are attempting great things, even though they fall.*
>
> SENECA,
> *On the Happy Life*

The first book of Marcus Aurelius's *Meditations* is a long list of the important people in his life, along with the virtues he observed in each of them. There is an interesting section where he writes about Claudius Maximus, a Stoic philosopher who served as his teacher. Marcus Aurelius doesn't mention Maximus's lectures, or any of the things usually associated with a teacher. Instead, the focus is solely on actions. Maximus was a role model because of the wisdom in the way he behaved, not because of the way he spoke in the classroom.

On Maximus: Doing your job without whining. [...] Generosity, charity, honesty. The sense he gave of staying on the path rather than being kept on it.

MARCUS AURELIUS,
Meditations, 1.15

Good role models are priceless. The mere act of watching the wise can expand our wisdom more than a thousand hours of lectures or pages in a book. The examples they provide should be cherished and deeply appreciated. Seneca would've approved of the way Einstein acted toward his role models: with heartfelt gratitude.

Unless we are complete ingrates, the lives of those men that preceded us should be seen as sacred. Their collective existence paved the way for our own time on Earth.

SENECA,
On the Shortness of Life

Lesson 39

THE POWER OF REMINDERS

*Use reminders to practice Stoicism
more effectively.*

The Battle of Waterloo in June 1815 marked the end of Napoleon Bonaparte's rule as Emperor of the French. He was forced to a hurried retreat from the battlefield to avoid being captured, leaving behind a carriage filled with personal belongings. The carriage was seized by Prussian soldiers and many of Napoleon's possessions were never again seen. One item in particular, which Napoleon carried with him to all battles during his time as emperor, was located 130 years later with a Dutch art collector living not too far from Waterloo. This item is known as the Talisman of Napoleon Bonaparte. It is a small crystal sculpture of a sphinx, just a few inches in length, decorated with 114 precious jewels. The origins of this piece of art are mysterious. It is believed that Napoleon commissioned the Italian sculptor Antonio Canova to create it in 1802, after Napoleon returned to France from a successful military excursion in Egypt. At Napoleon's request, the sculptor designed it with many symbolic elements. The jewels are arranged based on tarot code, following a numerology that alludes to Napoleon's military and political successes. The face of the sphinx was made to resemble Napoleon's wife, Joséphine de Beauharnais. It is full of customizations that make of it a unique and personal piece.

Some have described the talisman as an ostentatious eccentricity of a man known for his illusions of grandeur. Others have explained it in the light of Napoleon's documented mysticism, including his belief in omens and good luck charms. We will never know Napoleon's real motivations for commissioning the talisman. What we do know for certain is that he cherished it deeply. The symbolism of its design indicates that Napoleon carried it as a memento—a reminder of his accomplishments, his love for his wife, the values and principles that had made him so successful. These reminders gave him strength during the forty battles—thirty-five of them victories—in which he carried the talisman with him.

History is filled with similar examples of helpful reminders. Napoleon's talisman isn't different from the tattoos on the hands of Roman legionnaires. Or the poetry written by Cleanthes, Zeno's successor as head of the Stoic school in Athens. Or the Five Precepts at the core of Buddhism, or the Ten Commandments in Abrahamic religions. They all serve as reminders of a greater ideal. They can come in different levels of symbolism and offer varying degrees of explicit guidance, but always offer valuable support. Modern psychological research in the areas of self-control, memory, and decision-making shows that people who utilize reminders are overwhelmingly more likely to follow through with their objectives. This is another area where modern studies validate the beliefs of the ancient Stoic masters. They were fans of the power of reminders and wrote about several different ways of utilizing them in the practice of Stoicism.

1. Sententia. Seneca was a master of *sententiae*: brief expressions of conventional wisdom such as proverbs, adages, or maxims. No one has ever described the Stoic definition of poverty better than him: "It is not the man who has too little, but the man who craves more, that is poor." His aphorism about *memento mori* is timeless: "That man lives badly who does not know how to die well." Seneca understood the power of *sententiae*. He knew that when it came to philosophical lessons, a clever, concise description of a thought could be more compelling than a full lecture.

> *Individual aphorisms in a small compass, rounded off in units rather like lines of verse, become fixed more readily in the mind.*
>
> Seneca,
> *Moral Epistles, Letter 33*

This understanding of the value of *sententiae* is widespread across Stoic literature. Life can be complicated; things happen fast, changes catch us off guard. Having a summarized "go-to" list of wise lessons can be extremely helpful during turbulent times. Marcus Aurelius referred to his list as "epithets for yourself."

> *Epithets for yourself: Upright. Modest. Straightforward. Sane. Cooperative. Disinterested. Try not to exchange them for others. And if you should forfeit them, set about getting them back.*
>
> Marcus Aurelius,
> *Meditations, 10.8*

A good *sententia* serves as a mnemonic device to whoever creates it and to those who learn from it. This didactic quality of reminders is utilized by many religions and schools of thought. Mantras are central elements in Hinduism and Buddhism. Japanese history was heavily influenced by lists of precepts such as the Bushido, the moral code of Samurai behavior, and the Seventeen-Article Constitution, a seventh-century document outlining the morals expected of government officials. The most famous Stoic list of precepts comes from book 11, section 18 of *Meditations*. This section is often referred to as the Stoic Ten Commandments, where Marcus Aurelius lists ten lessons that he believed should always be kept in mind.

> i. That we came into the world for the sake of one another.
> ii. How people are driven by their beliefs.
> iii. If they're right to do this, then you have no right to com-

plain. And if they aren't, then they do it involuntarily.
iv. You've made enough mistakes yourself.
v. A lot of things are means to some other end.
vi. Human life is very short. Before long all of us will be laid out side by side.
vii. It's not what they do that bothers us. It's our misperceptions.
viii. How much more damage anger and grief do than the things that cause them.
ix. Kindness is invincible.
x. To expect bad people not to injure others is crazy. It's to ask the impossible.

MARCUS AURELIUS,
Meditations, 11.18

2. Literature. René Descartes, whose philosophy shared many elements with Stoicism, wrote a beautiful description of the allure of literature in his philosophical tour de force *Discourse on the Method*:

The reading of all good books is indeed like a conversation with the noblest men of past centuries who were the authors of them, or rather a carefully studied conversation, in which they reveal to us none but the best of their thoughts.

RENÉ DESCARTES,
Discourse on the Method, Part 1

Marcus Aurelius, Seneca, Epictetus, and even Zeno are accessible through the pages of a book. The best way to memorize the teachings of Stoicism is to frequently read the works of these Stoic masters. Many Stoic books have been written with the purpose of transforming more abstruse philosophical topics into actionable items for everyday life. The most notable example is Epictetus's

Enchiridion, which was compiled by his student Arrian as a practical handbook of advice. The *Enchiridion* served as inspiration for me to write *The Stoic Arsenal*. Most of Seneca's essays are letters to his close friends, where he tried to apply Stoic teachings to routine events. Seneca advised his friend Lucilius to develop the habit of rereading the works of his favorite authors.

> *You should be extending your stay among writers whose genius is unquestionable, deriving constant nourishment from them if you wish to gain anything from your reading that will find a lasting place in your mind. To be everywhere is to be nowhere. Nothing is so useful that it can be of any service in the mere passing.*
>
> Seneca,
Moral Epistles, Letter 2

3. *Meditation*. The term *meditation* is notoriously elusive to define. It can refer to mindfulness-based practices that derive from Buddhism. In a Christian context, it is used to describe contemplative prayers. Those who practice tai chi chuan are familiar with the concept of movement meditation. The common characteristic across these practices is that *meditation* is used to describe an action where one engages in contemplation or reflection.

Stoic meditation is one more flavor of meditative practice. It consists of setting aside a dedicated time to reflect on current events and analyze them through the lenses of Stoicism. Marcus Aurelius chose to do this in the morning, after waking up. He would use the time to reflect on which Stoic lessons would help him the most during the upcoming events of the day. By doing this, he would prepare himself for his daily challenges and go into them with a preset mindset on how to act. Lesson 21 talked about how he used this technique to prepare himself to interact with unethical people.

> *When you wake up in the morning, tell yourself: The people I deal with today will be meddling, ungrateful, arrogant, dishonest, jealous, surly. They are like this because they can't tell good from evil.*
>
> MARCUS AURELIUS,
Meditations, 2.1

Seneca preferred to meditate at night. He would reflect on the occurrences of the day and keep mental notes on areas where he hadn't acted according to Stoic teachings. All his actions—both good and bad—were scrutinized, as if he were being interrogated by a judge.

> *The mind must be called to account every day. This was Sextius' practice: when the day was spent and he had retired to his night's rest, he asked his mind, "Which of your ills did you heal today? Which vice did you resist? In what aspect are you better?" Your anger will cease and become more controllable if it knows that every day it must come before a judge. [...] I exercise this jurisdiction daily and plead my case before myself.*
>
> SENECA,
On Anger

Epictetus had a meditation routine similar to Seneca's. He also meditated at night about the events of the day.

> *Admit not sleep into your tender eyelids, till you have reckoned up each deed of the day. How have I erred, what done or left undone? So start, and so review your acts, and then for vile deeds chide yourself, for good be glad.*
>
> EPICTETUS,
Discourses, 3.10

4. Artifacts. Physical objects are the most literal forms of reminders. Several types of objects have been used over time to represent Stoic teachings: coins, amulets, charms, paintings, statues, just to name a few. The *vanitas* style of painting is known for its motifs related to *memento mori*. Michel de Montaigne carved a quote from Epictetus into the wooden beams of his personal library: "that which worries men are not things but that which they think about them." Seneca was an art collector and kept sculptures of role models he admired.

> *Why shouldn't I keep images of great men beside me, to stir my mind to action, and even celebrate their birthdays? Why shouldn't I address them by name each time, as a way to honor them? The same homage I render to my teachers, I owe also to the teachers of the human race, who are the source of so much good.*
>
> Seneca,
Moral Epistles, Letter 64

Stoic reminders can come in innumerous varieties, but their purpose is always the same: to help us recall the teachings that improve the quality of our lives. By utilizing reminders, we can always keep the most valuable Stoic lessons within arm's reach of memory.

Lesson 40

CREATE A NEW PATH

Improve Stoicism with new ideas.

In the initial years after its founding, Stoicism had a different name. Those who walked in the ancient *agora* of Athens and saw the group of philosophy students gathered in front of the Stoa Poikile referred to the school as Zenonism. It was common for Greek schools of philosophy to be named after their founders; Epicureanism came from Epicurus, Platonism from Plato, Pyrrhonism from Pyrrho. But the early Stoics decided that naming their school after Zeno of Citium might lead to undesirable side consequences. There were two main concerns. First, they feared that it could create a cult of personality around Zeno. Second, and most importantly, naming the school after an individual would go against a core teaching of Stoic philosophy. Stoicism makes an explicit claim that no one is perfectly wise. The founders of the school desired to be seen as men in search of wisdom, not as flawless sages. They recognized that their teachings would likely evolve with time. They accepted the possibility that future generations might see their ideas as antiquated. Therefore, it seemed unwise to tie the name of their philosophy to someone whose teachings could potentially become obsolete. This humble attitude of not only embracing improvements, but expecting them, became part of Stoicism's DNA. It is certainly one of the main reasons why Stoicism remains relevant after more than two millennia.

1. Innovation. Stoic openness to innovation derives from it not being constricted by a claim of absolute wisdom. The Stoic teachers from the past gave their students full latitude to propose improvements. The philosophy gradually changed as it incorporated new ideas and adapted to different times and cultures. The Stoicism of the early Greek Stoics such as Zeno, Cleanthes, and Chrysippus was markedly different from that of the late Roman Stoics such as Seneca, Epictetus, and Marcus Aurelius. The early Stoics emphasized the study of physics and logic, while the late Stoics placed most of the focus on ethics and its relationship to human psychology. The Neostoicism of the Renaissance brought in elements of Christianity, while the modern Stoicism of the contemporary era is more secular and influenced by advancements in cognitive psychotherapy. Seneca wrote about how philosophy is made better by this process of continuous change.

> *The vitality of Philosophy is strengthened by each new generation's contributions to it. The Philosopher alone is unfettered by the confines of humanity but lives forever, like a god. He embraces memory, utilizes the present and anticipates with relish what is to come. He makes his time on Earth longer by merging past, present and future into one.*
>
> Seneca,
> *On the Shortness of Life*

Out of the main Roman Stoics, Seneca was the most explicit about his detachment from prior teachings. In one of his most famous passages, he described how he felt total liberty to propose new ideas.

> *Yes indeed, I shall use the old road, but if I find a shorter and easier one I shall open it up. The men who pioneered the old routes are leaders, not our masters. Truth lies open to every-*

one. There has yet to be a monopoly of truth. And there is plenty of it left for future generations too.

SENECA,
Moral Epistles, Letter 33

Not only did he seek ways to innovate, but he criticized those who failed to do so.

It is disgraceful that a man who is old or in sight of old age should have wisdom deriving solely from his notebook. 'Zeno said this.' And what have you said? 'Cleanthes said that.' What have you said? How much longer are you going to serve under others' orders? Assume authority yourself and utter something that may be handed down to posterity. Produce something from your own resources.

SENECA,
Moral Epistles, Letter 33

Seneca knew that his deviations from more standard teachings could result in something worse. Lesson 35 includes a quote where he recognizes his faults and even compares himself to someone lying in a hospital bed while giving advice to other sick patients. But he understood that the other Stoic teachers were fallible human beings just like him. He saw them as wise peers, not as all-knowing gods.

We are in search of truth in company with the very men that teach it.

SENECA,
On Leisure

2. **Independence.** It is easy to see why Seneca was drawn to the independence that Stoicism grants to its followers. He was used to

the Roman Senate—a place known for fierce debates and unsteady loyalties. In his essay *On Leisure*, he made an observation to his friend Serenus on this topic.

> *If a man always follows the opinion of one person, his place is not in senate, but in a faction.*
>
> SENECA,
On Leisure

He didn't constrain this view to politics. It should apply to all areas of inquiry where ideas are debated.

> *I do not bind myself to some particular one of the Stoic masters; I, too, have the right to form an opinion.*
>
> SENECA,
On the Happy Life

Stoicism is an open forum. New generations are welcomed to sit alongside the teachers of the past. A Stoic has freedom to propose new ideas.

> *Whom should we attribute them [Stoic teachings] to? Zeno? Cleanthes? Chrysippus? Panaetius? Posidonius? We Stoics are no monarch's subjects; each asserts his own freedom.*
>
> SENECA,
Moral Epistles, Letter 33

Independence is key for innovation. Without it, a philosophy remains chained to the past while the rest of society evolves.

> *People who never attain independence follow the views of their predecessors, first, in matters in which everyone else without exception has abandoned the older authority con-*

cerned, secondly, in matters in which investigations are still not complete. But no new findings will ever be made if we rest content with the findings of the past.

Seneca,
Moral Epistles, Letter 33

The final teaching in this book is arguably also the most important. Civilization is a walk toward new discoveries that bring fresh perspectives to old problems and solve mysteries from the past. The founders of Stoicism had the foresight to leave the philosophy open to these improvements. It is up to us to ensure that Stoicism continues evolving. For our benefit and that of future generations.

Selected Bibliography

Alford, Brad A., and Aaron T. Beck. *The Integrative Power of Cognitive Therapy.* New York: The Guilford Press, 1998.

Aristotle. *Aristotle's Nicomachean Ethics.* Translated by Robert C. Bartlett and Susan D. Collins. Chicago: The University of Chicago Press, 2012.

Aurelius, Marcus. *Meditations.* Translated by Gregory Hays. New York: Modern Library, 2003.

Beck, Aaron T., A. John Rush, Brian E. Shaw, and Gary Emery. *Cognitive Therapy of Depression.* New York: The Guilford Press, 1987.

Becker, Lawrence C. *A New Stoicism.* Princeton, NJ: Princeton University Press, 2017.

Durant, Will. *The Story of Philosophy.* New York: Simon & Schuster, 2005.

Ellis, Albert. *Reason and Emotion in Psychotherapy.* New York: Lyle Stuart, 1963.

Epictetus. *Discourses and Selected Writings.* Translated by Robert Dobbin. New York: Penguin, 2008.

Farnsworth, Ward. *The Practicing Stoic.* Boston: David R. Godine, 2018.

Frankl, Viktor E. *Man's Search for Meaning.* Boston: Beacon Press, 2016.

Hadot, Pierre. *Philosophy as a Way of Life.* Translated by Michael Chase. Malden, MA: Blackwell Publishers, 1995.

Hadot, Pierre. *The Inner Citadel.* Translated by Michael Chase. Cambridge, MA: Harvard University Press, 2001.

Holiday, Ryan. *Stillness Is the Key.* New York: Portfolio/Penguin, 2019.

Holiday, Ryan. *The Obstacle Is the Way: The Timeless Art of Turning Trials into Triumph.* New York: Portfolio/Penguin, 2014.

Irvine, William B. *A Guide to the Good Life.* Oxford: Oxford University Press, 2009.

King, Cynthia. *Musonius Rufus: Lectures and Sayings.* CreateSpace, 2011.

Lefcourt, Herbert M., and Rod A. Martin. *Humor and Life Stress: Antidote to Adversity.* New York: Springer, 2011.

Pigliucci, Massimo, and Gregory Lopez. *A Handbook for New Stoics.* New York: The Experiment, 2019.

Plato. *The Last Days of Socrates: Euthyphro, Apology, Crito, Phaedo.* London: Penguin, 2003.

Robertson, Donald. *How to Think Like a Roman Emperor.* New York: St. Martin's Press, 2019.

Seneca, Lucius A. *Anger, Mercy, Revenge.* Translated by Robert Kaster and Martha Nussbaum. Chicago: The University of Chicago Press, 2010.

Seneca, Lucius A. *Letters from a Stoic.* Translated by Richard Mott Gummere. Adansonia Publishing, 2018.

Seneca, Lucius A. *Letters from a Stoic.* Translated by Robin Campbell. London: Penguin, 2004.

Seneca, Lucius A. *Letters on Ethics.* Translated by Margaret Graver and A. A. Long. Chicago: The University of Chicago Press, 2015.

Seneca, Lucius A. *On Benefits.* Translated by Miriam Griffin and Brad Inwood. Chicago: The University of Chicago Press, 2011.

Seneca, Lucius A. *On Consolation to Helvia, Marcia, and Polybius.* Translated by Frank Miller, 1917. Independently published.

Seneca, Lucius A. *On Leisure.* Translated by Frank Miller. Cambridge, MA: Harvard University Press, 1917.

Seneca, Lucius A. *On Providence.* Translated by Aubrey Stewart, 1900. Independently published.

Seneca, Lucius A. *On the Firmness of the Wise Person.* Translated by Aubrey Stewart, 1900. Independently published.

Seneca, Lucius A. *On the Happy Life.* Translated by Aubrey Stewart, 1900. Independently published.

Seneca, Lucius A. *On the Shortness of Life.* Translated by Damian Stevenson, 2018. Independently published.

Seneca, Lucius A. *On the Tranquility of the Mind.* Translated by Aubrey Stewart, 1900. Independently published.

Yourcenar, Marguerite. *Memoirs of Hadrian.* Translated by Grace Frick. New York: Farrar, Straus, and Giroux, 2005.

www.ingramcontent.com/pod-product-compliance
Lightning Source LLC
LaVergne TN
LVHW011811060526
838200LV00053B/3735